T0063647

I Am a Christian

Discovering What It Means to Follow Jesus
Together with Fellow Believers

†

I
Am A
Christian

THOM S. RAINER

TYNDALE
MOMENTUM®

A Tyndale nonfiction imprint

Visit Tyndale online at tyndale.com.

Visit Tyndale Momentum online at tyndalemomentum.com.

Tyndale, Tyndale's quill logo, *Tyndale Momentum*, and the Tyndale Momentum logo are registered trademarks of Tyndale House Ministries. Tyndale Momentum is a nonfiction imprint of Tyndale House Publishers, Carol Stream, Illinois.

I Am a Christian: Discovering What It Means to Follow Jesus Together with Fellow Believers

The Author is represented by Alive Literary Agency, www.aliveliterary.com.

Designed by Eva M. Winters.

For information about special discounts for bulk purchases, please contact Tyndale House Publishers at csresponse@tyndale.com, or call 1-855-277-9400.

Library of Congress Cataloging-in-Publication Data

A catalog record for this book is available from the Library of Congress.

ISBN 978-1-4964-4892-7

Printed in the United States of America

28	27	26	25	24	23	22
7	6	5	4	3	2	1

To Amy Jordan and Jana Biesecker.
Two incredible leaders at Church Answers.
Two incredible friends to me.

And always to Nellie Jo.
Your gentle nudge led me to a church when I was a young man.
Your persistent love sustains me and
strengthens me as an old man.

CONTENTS

ACKNOWLEDGMENTS

I did not expect a business meeting in Franklin, Tennessee, to become one of the most momentous events of my life. When Ron Beers and Jon Farrar of Tyndale House Publishers came to talk to me about writing some books, I thought it would be just another meeting, but it was so much more. It was the beginning of both a professional relationship and an exceptional friendship.

I soon met Jan Long Harris as well, and these three Tyndale leaders have become friends I know I will cherish for life.

Without a doubt, the entire Tyndale team has been a blessing to me. Ron, Jon, and Jan started the relationship, but it has expanded to include many more.

Thank you, Bryan Norman of Alive Literary. Though I've written more than thirty books, you are my first agent. You have demonstrated your worth, class, and acumen again and again. I am incredibly blessed by you.

The team at Church Answers includes several family members, but even those who aren't Rainers are like family to me. I love working with you. I love the joy, laughter, and passion you have for churches and church leaders. I can't imagine serving alongside anyone else.

I absolutely love my family. I love my wife, Nellie Jo. I love our sons, Sam, Art, and Jess. I love Erin, Sarah, and Rachel, our daughters-in-law. And I love our eleven (and counting) grandchildren. If you know anything about me, you know how much my family means to me. My world is first Christ and then my family. Did I mention that I love my family?

This book represents my greatest passion in ministry. Its thesis is simple. We who are Christians should know *why* we are Christians and why we should live out our faith in the context of a local church. Churches and church leaders often get a bad rap these days. It is now in vogue to criticize both and disparage their importance.

From the first local church in Jerusalem to the millions of churches around the world today, God is still at work in local congregations. In our walk as Christians, we need to remember the importance of the local church for our growth and effectiveness in the faith.

You may be reading this book in a new members or discipleship class, in a small group, or on your own. I have two messages for you. First, thank you for picking up a book with a common but curious title and deciding to take the time to read it. Second, I am praying that God will use this book to help you understand more fully what it means to follow Christ. I am praying that you will clearly see and embrace how God intends for you to live out your faith—in the community and context of a local church.

The title of this book, *I Am a Christian,* is a great statement with deep meaning.

May it be a powerful statement for you as well.

Thom S. Rainer
Franklin, Tennessee

WHO AM I?

A common icebreaker in new groups is to ask everyone to share something about themselves that nobody else would know. Maybe it's something their spouse would know, but sometimes even spouses are surprised by what is revealed.

On one such occasion, I responded, "I was a fifth-generation banker." It's possible that a few people in the room knew I started my work life as a banker, but hardly anyone knew I carried on a family legacy spanning five generations. It might be even more surprising to learn that all three of my sons were sixth-generation bankers before they answered the call to vocational ministry.

So, who am I today?

I am the husband of Nellie Jo; the father of Sam, Art,

and Jess; and the granddad of Canon, Will, Harper, Collins, Nathaniel, Joshua, James, Maggie, Bren, Joel, and Dominic. (That's the present tally, at least.) I am the son of Sam and Nan and the brother of Sam and Amy. (Yes, we like the name Sam in my family.)

Who am I? I am the friend of many people who have blessed my life immeasurably. My friends have been there for me in the good times and the tough times. I hope I have been that type of friend to them as well.

Who am I? I am the leader of Church Answers. I am the author of a lot of books. I have been the dean of a seminary and the pastor of four churches.

In short, I identify as a family man, a friend, a sports enthusiast, an author, and a person who has served in vocational ministry for a long time.

But who am I really?

If we were playing the icebreaker game right now and I asked you to identify yourself in one comprehensive sentence, what would you say?

I haven't always been as bold and forthcoming as I'd like to be, but if you asked me that question today, my response would be, "I am a Christian."

What exactly does that mean?

For certain, it means I have confessed that I am a sinner. I have repented of my sins and placed my faith in Jesus Christ. I believe that his death on the cross was on my behalf. He took the punishment I deserve. He is my sacrifice, my Savior, my Lord, and my King.

To say that I am a Christian means I have chosen to center my life in the person of Jesus Christ. He is my hope and my salvation. He is my present. He is my eternity. Simply stated, he is my all. And though I am far from perfect in how I live my life and share my faith, my desire is always to openly proclaim Jesus and identify myself with him.

"I am a Christian" means I have a new identity—indeed a *powerful* new identity—in Christ. In the following pages, I will unpack the meaning of this simple, four-word sentence. Though the statement is brief, the implications are far-reaching, lifesaving, and life-changing.

THE URGENCY OF THE MOMENT

In today's culture, many false belief systems are vying for our hearts and minds. The conflict can be both confusing and overwhelming. Right now, perhaps more than at any other time in history, we need to understand the urgency of the moment. So many forces in our culture seek to grab our time, attention, and commitment. Whether it's politics, sports, leisure, social media, or the latest issue of the day, there is no shortage of opportunities to get involved. To be clear, these opportunities are not all bad. But they can cause us to forget our true purpose in life as followers of Christ: to rescue lost souls and change the world for the better. At this pivotal moment, when our culture seems to teeter between one direction or another, we need to claim our most important identity—follower of Christ—and act on it.

DISTRACTIONS THAT DIVIDE AND CONQUER

Two hours before boarding a connecting flight home, I arrived at the busy airport too weary to read or work. So instead I simply sat in a chair near the gate and observed people.

I was amazed by how many people walked with their heads down, staring at their smartphones, and it struck me how quickly smartphones have changed our culture. We are on distraction overload with no end in sight.

I recently spoke to a man who is deeply concerned about how busy his family has become. For reasons he couldn't explain, he and his wife feel compelled to keep their three young children in sports year-round. Whenever they take a family vacation, it is filled with activities. They are involved in countless events at school. They are caught up in social media.

"We are too busy to enjoy life and each other," the young father lamented. "Activities control us. My wife and I spend more time on social media than reading the Bible. It's pathetic."

This is not something that can just be cleaned up around

the edges. Embracing our identity as Christians means we must shift our priorities—both for ourselves and for our families. The subtle siren call of busyness is hurting many families and damaging people's lives. Our world needs a revolution of peace and restfulness that only Christ can provide. We have an opportunity to exemplify the abundant life that Jesus promised us, but not if we keep chasing after the world. Instead, we must grasp the significance of our identity in Christ. We must grab hold of what it really means to say, "I am a Christian."

"Be still, and know that I am God! I will be honored by every nation. I will be honored throughout the world" (Psalm 46:10).

Hear those words. Heed those words. Slow down. Eliminate distractions. The time is now.

I AM A CHRISTIAN IN THE CHURCH

Then Came Bronson was a short-lived television series in 1969 and 1970 about a young businessman who quits his job and wanders from town to town on his Harley-Davidson motorcycle. The impetus for this dramatic change in his life was the suicide of his friend. The series was intended to stir our emotions about what really matters in life.

Instead, the show became a template for the illusory "good life." What if we could just wander around the country, free as a bird? The life of a loner was held up as an ideal for many to seek.

But that is not God's plan for us. From the very beginning, with Adam, God declared, "It is not good for the man to be alone. I will make a helper who is just right for him" (Genesis 2:18). The entire Old Testament is about how God called a people to himself. We are meant to live in community.

That theme continues in the New Testament. In the four Gospels, we see Jesus surround himself with people. We see that his ministry and mission are focused on others—reconciling them to a relationship with God. "For the Son of Man came to seek and save those who are lost" (Luke 19:10).

The book of Acts tells the story of Christ's ascension and Peter's subsequent sermon on the Day of Pentecost. And what happens after that sermon? Through the work of the Holy Spirit, God's people immediately come together and a local church is formed in Jerusalem.

Once again, we see God's plan for Christians to gather, work, serve, and love others together. Just as it wasn't good for the first man, Adam, to be alone, it is not good for Christians to be alone.

From the second chapter of Acts to the early chapters of Revelation, we read the stories of local churches on a mission. Local churches striving for unity. Local churches teaching the gospel. Local churches serving others in their communities.

Lone Ranger Christianity is not biblical Christianity. God gave us local churches to carry out his mission. It is *his* plan. It is *his* purpose.

When Christians become committed church members, the church becomes healthy. When the church becomes healthy, communities become healthy. When communities become healthy, the world is transformed.

The urgent need of our day is for Christians to become committed church members. Sure, our churches are imperfect, and so are we as Christians. The Bible doesn't hide those realities. But it is amazing and miraculous what God will do through a few devoted Christians who become committed and selfless church members.

It is true that churches in North America are declining. But maybe we're missing a bigger story in this sad reality. Perhaps the issue is not declining churches, but the declining commitment of Christians. Perhaps the story is one of declining faith.

In other parts of the world, millions of Christians are gathering with a commitment to Christ that manifests as a commitment to the local church. They gather ready to serve, give, and evangelize. Some gather at great risk to their lives. But they know how important the gathered church is. They will continue to gather and demonstrate faith, even if it costs them dearly.

The local church is God's plan. We must become part of

his plan. We must serve through our local churches. "I am a Christian" and "I am a church member" go hand in hand.

THE SEVEN "I AM" STATEMENTS OF JESUS

The seven chapters of this book will cover seven "I am" statements that are part and parcel of what it means to declare, "I am a Christian." Before we start that journey, let's take a brief look at seven "I am" statements that Jesus used. Each one is a clear echo of the decisive statement God used to reveal himself to Moses centuries earlier: "I AM WHO I AM" (Exodus 3:14). Jesus used the same phrase to assert his identity and affirm that he is God.

"I Am the Bread of Life"

When the crowds around Jesus insisted that he perform a miracle like the manna that fell in the wilderness to feed the people of Israel, Jesus replied, "I am the bread of life. Whoever comes to me will never be hungry again. Whoever believes in me will never be thirsty" (John 6:35).

Of course, Jesus was speaking of something greater than physical and temporal sustenance. The "bread" he spoke of provided eternal spiritual nourishment. No one who accepts him as their bread of life will ever be spiritually lacking again.

"I Am the Light of the World"

In the passage following Jesus' encounter with the woman caught in adultery, we find these powerful words: "Jesus spoke to the people once more and said, 'I am the light of the world. If you follow me, you won't have to walk in darkness, because you will have the light that leads to life'" (John 8:12).

Light is a metaphor commonly used to describe the three persons of the Trinity: Father, Son, and Holy Spirit. Jesus was emphatic that he and God the Father are one. As God the Father is light, so is Jesus. He provides a way in the darkness that no one else can provide.

"I Am the Gate for the Sheep"

The metaphor of a shepherd with his sheep is one that Jesus used often. He described himself as one who watched over and protected his sheep sacrificially. He always put his sheep before himself. He told the crowd in John 10:7, "I tell you the truth, I am the gate for the sheep."

This verse has two powerful meanings. First, those who come to God through the gate (Jesus) will be his sheep. They will be saved. Second, as a shepherd, Jesus guards the gate of the fold where his sheep are resting. No one will get to them or take them away. They will be safe.

"I Am the Good Shepherd"

A good shepherd sacrificially protects his sheep. "A hired hand will run when he sees a wolf coming. He will abandon the sheep because they don't belong to him and he isn't their shepherd. And so the wolf attacks them and scatters the flock" (John 10:12). But the good shepherd does more. "The good shepherd sacrifices his life for the sheep" (John 10:11).

Though few understood the true meaning of Jesus' words before he went to the cross, those who witnessed Jesus' crucifixion saw how the Good Shepherd sacrificed his life for his sheep. His immeasurable love for us is completely sacrificial.

"I Am the Resurrection and the Life"

Jesus conquered death. Think about that statement. Without the Resurrection, we would be without hope.

Speaking to his friend Martha, Jesus said, "I am the resurrection and the life. Anyone who believes in me will live, even after dying" (John 11:25).

Jesus then emphasized this truth to Martha: "Everyone who lives in me and believes in me will never ever die. Do you believe this, Martha?"

"Yes, Lord" (John 11:26-27).

How about *you*? Do you believe this?

"I Am the Way, the Truth, and the Life"

There is only one way of salvation. Look at Jesus' words in John 14:6: "I am the way, the truth, and the life. No one can come to the Father except through me."

We refer to this truth as the *doctrine of exclusivity*. It simply means that there is no other way to salvation except through faith in Jesus. Jesus was clear and unequivocal on this point.

"I Am the True Vine"

Those who follow Christ are saved by grace through faith (Ephesians 2:8-9). And those who truly put their faith in Christ will bear fruit (Ephesians 2:10). Good works are not what save us; but if we have truly placed our faith in Christ, we will do the works God has called us to do.

Jesus used the metaphor of the vine and the gardener to explain this truth in John 15:1-2: "I am the true grapevine, and my Father is the gardener. He cuts off every branch of mine that doesn't produce fruit, and he prunes the branches that do bear fruit so they will produce even more."

Jesus' seven "I am" statements are succinct but powerful. They make it clear who Jesus is and what his life, death, and resurrection mean. For the remainder of this book, we will turn our attention to seven "I am" statements essential to being a Christian. All followers of Jesus must fully grasp what it means to say, "I am a Christian."

DISCUSSION QUESTIONS

1. Christians, sadly, can give more value to other identities in their lives than to the identity of being a Christian. What are some of the competing identities in the lives of Christians?

2. Read John 14:6 again. What does the doctrine of exclusivity mean?

3. Why is it so important for Christians to be fully and selflessly committed to their local church? What does the Bible say about "loner Christianity"?

I AM A BELIEVER

My mother had an incredible sense of humor, though she often didn't have a filter to determine when and where to express it. Actually, her humor shone through the brightest in some of those awkward moments.

After my dad died, I tried to get Mom to visit us as often as possible. Because it was a long drive from her home to ours, I would fly to her town, and we would fly back together. The first time we did this, Mom had not been on an airplane in many years. To give you an idea, the last time she had flown, she just walked onto the plane with her paper ticket in hand. Obviously, times have changed.

I forewarned my mom that she would have to provide identification to get through security. She thought that was silly. At one point, I thought our trip would be scuttled by her refusal. But Mom knew her grandchildren awaited her, and she would sacrifice anything for those three boys.

Still, she felt burdened to point out to the frazzled ticket agent the absurdity of asking for identification. The conversation is etched in my memory.

"Why do I need identification?"

"Because we have to verify you are you, ma'am."

"Well, that's silly. Who do you *think* I am?"

"I don't know who you are, ma'am, until I see your ID."

"Well, I could have just introduced myself."

The ticket agent sighed and returned my mom's driver's license to her.

Unfortunately, Mom couldn't let it rest.

"You know, that's not really me in the photo."

At this point, I could tell the agent was losing his patience. I told my mom that it was indeed her photo. But she had to have the last word.

"Well, that's a horrendous picture. It's not me. I know who I am."

I gently put my hand under her elbow and escorted her toward security. All the while, she continued to insist, "I know who I am."

We have an identity as Christians. We sometimes call ourselves *believers*. Thus, what we have in common with other

Christians are what we call *beliefs*. To say, "I am a Christian," means we hold to some common truths.

Let's take a moment to examine several of those foundational beliefs.

PRIMARY PRINCIPLES

Because our leadership conference was supposed to include hands-on instruction, we limited the attendance to fifty people. So I didn't expect the denominational diversity we ended up with. There were Baptists, Presbyterians, Methodists, Wesleyans, Nazarenes, and Assemblies of God. Within some of those groups, more than one affiliated denomination was represented. On top of that, twenty-one attendees identified themselves as nondenominational.

With that much diversity across the theological spectrum, I wondered whether I could get us all on the same page doctrinally before we proceeded to look at practical ministry matters. Though we definitely had our differences on secondary and tertiary issues, I was amazed—and gratified—to find enthusiastic agreement about the primary issues of Christian faith.

The Bible Is the Word of God

Without believing in the truthfulness of the Bible, it would be difficult to affirm the rest of our beliefs. After all, we learn from the Bible about Creation, the Fall, the nature of God, the work of the Holy Spirit, the person of Christ, the reality of Christ's death on the cross, the Resurrection, and the coming return of Christ.

God revealed himself through Jesus Christ, "the Word . . . made flesh" (John 1:14, KJV). And God revealed himself through the Word of God, which we call the Bible.

Scripture affirms itself as God's revealed Word. As the apostle Paul wrote to Timothy, "All Scripture is inspired by God and is useful to teach us what is true and to make us realize what is wrong in our lives. It corrects us when we are wrong and teaches us to do what is right" (2 Timothy 3:16).

In the original language of the New Testament, the word *inspired* here means "breathed." In fact, in many English translations of the Bible, the word is translated as "God-breathed." The Bible is the very breath of God. It is completely true.

If we begin to doubt the truth of any portion of Scripture, we undermine our confidence that any other part is true as well. If we decide for ourselves what is true in the Bible and what is not, we're essentially shaping our doctrine and beliefs to match our own whims and desires.

Because the Bible is both God-given and God-inspired, it is able to accomplish God's purpose of drawing us to salvation and teaching us how to live as Christians. The writer of Hebrews forcefully articulates the potency of Scripture:

"For the word of God is alive and powerful. It is sharper than the sharpest two-edged sword, cutting between soul and spirit, between joint and marrow. It exposes our innermost thoughts and desires" (Hebrews 4:12).

When we affirm that all of the Bible is true, we allow God to shape our beliefs. It is foundational for us to accept the truthfulness of all of Scripture.

There Is One God, in Three Persons

There is only one God. He is the creator of all. He is sovereign over all. He is omnipotent (all-powerful), omniscient (all-knowing), and omnipresent (not limited by space and time). This one God reveals himself to us as three persons: Father, Son, and Holy Spirit. Frankly, the issue of the Trinity is one of the more challenging doctrines to understand. But if I believe that Jesus was raised from the dead, which I emphatically do, I can believe in the Trinitarian God even if I don't fully understand the details.

God the Father reigns supreme over the universe. He is all-loving, all-wise, and completely just. He becomes a Father to those who, by faith, accept his Son, Jesus Christ. This truth is one of the greatest points of security I have. God loves me as his child.

Jesus Christ is the eternal Son of God. Conceived by the Holy Spirt and born of a virgin named Mary, he came in the flesh to live among us.

Jesus lived a sinless life on earth. He willingly sacrificed his life on the cross for our sins. As our substitute, he took the punishment due to us. He was buried for three days in a borrowed tomb and then rose from the dead. Through his death and resurrection, all who believe in him will have eternal life in his presence.

In his last act on the earth, Jesus told his followers to be his witnesses. He then ascended to heaven and now reigns at the right hand of God the Father. One day, he will return to judge the world and establish his Kingdom.

The Holy Spirit is the third person of the Trinity. He inspired the writers many years ago to pen the words that make up the Bible. The Holy Spirit enables believers to understand truth. He exalts Christ. He convicts people of sin. He calls people to accept Jesus Christ as their Lord and Savior.

Humanity, the Fall, and Restoration

Men and women are created in the image of God. Adam and Eve's sin marred that image, creating an eternal separation between God and humanity. Every person is born in sin and needs forgiveness. God offers redemption and restoration to all who confess and repent of their sin and seek God's mercy and forgiveness through Jesus Christ, who took the punishment for our sin on the cross.

The Resurrection of Christ

"He is alive!" Those three words are a powerful affirmation of the foundations of our beliefs. We serve a God who is alive. In fact, the apostle Paul declared that the Christian faith would be futile without the Resurrection: "If there is no resurrection of the dead, then Christ has not been raised. And if Christ has not been raised, then your faith is useless and you are still guilty of your sins" (1 Corinthians 15:16-17).

Yes, the Resurrection is essential to the Christian faith. Paul minces no words. Without it, our faith is *useless*.

But there's more. The Resurrection assures us that Christ is alive and that we who are Christians will live forever with him in eternity. "But there is an order to this resurrection: Christ was raised as the first of the harvest; then all who belong to Christ will be raised when he comes back" (1 Corinthians 15:23).

Because he lives, we live as well. Such is the promise of the Resurrection.

Salvation

I recently read a news article in which a celebrity declared that, if there really is a heaven, he will definitely gain entrance. After all, he has done so many good things in his life that God will *have* to let him in. But the Bible does not teach salvation based on good works. To the contrary, if we're depending on our works to save us, we are in a lot of trouble!

John 3:16 is likely the most quoted verse in the Bible: "For this is how God loved the world: He gave his one and only Son, so that everyone who believes in him will not perish but have eternal life."

God created us in his image and loves us as his creation. But we messed up that perfect image through sin. God is holy and perfect, and he made a way for us to be perfect. It is through *his* work that we are saved, certainly not our own. Instead of us taking the punishment for our sins, God sent his one and only Son, Jesus, to die in our place. God does not desire for us to perish. He made a way for us to have eternal life.

Why did God provide this way? What was his motivation? After all, we humans rebelled against him. We don't deserve his salvation. Look again at the first phrase in John 3:16: "For this is how God loved the world." God's motivation was simple and pure—complete, unconditional love.

God, in his grace, offers us eternal life as a free gift. It must be received by faith. "God saved you by his grace when you believed. And you can't take credit for this; it is a gift from God. Salvation is not a reward for the good things we have done, so none of us can boast about it" (Ephesians 2:8-9).

When you declare, "I am a believer," you are certainly

affirming the truths we have covered in this chapter. But you're not merely believing in *something*; you're believing in *someone*. You have confessed and repented of your sinfulness. You have accepted the reality that Christ took your punishment on the cross. And by faith you have received the free gift of salvation.

I AM A BELIEVER WITH WORKS

When Paul concluded his first letter to the church at Corinth, he gave them five imperatives: "Be on guard. Stand firm in the faith. Be courageous. Be strong. And do everything with love" (1 Corinthians 16:13-14). The first two imperatives are closely tied to the affirmation, "I am a believer."

When Paul exhorts us to be on guard, he is warning us about error and heresy coming into the church. He wants us to be guardians of the truth God has given us.

But "stand firm in the faith" is an admonition for us not to drift from the faith. Yes, we are believers. But we must stand firm in what we believe. How do we do that? How do we go beyond mere mental assent to working out our belief? The answer is not formulaic, but it is clear in Scripture. Among the many ways we can stand firm in our faith are four imperatives we must not neglect: connect with others, read the Bible, prioritize prayer, and share what we believe. These works are not what save us, but our salvation must lead to works. As it says in James 2:14, "What good is it . . . if you say you have faith but don't show it by your actions? Can that kind of faith save anyone?" Further, unless our faith "produces good deeds, it is dead and useless" (James 2:17).

Connect with Others

The entire New Testament is written in the context of a community of believers. Ever since the first church was birthed in Jerusalem on the Day of Pentecost (see Acts 2), God's plan for his people has been for us to live out our faith in the community of others. The faith of Christian believers was never meant to be lived in solitude. Most books of the New Testament were written either to a church or to a church leader. Community brings encouragement. Community brings accountability. Community brings strength. Community brings hope.

If we want to stand firm in the faith, if we want to grow in the faith, we must do so in the context of other believers, specifically the local church. We will look at this issue more fully in the next chapter.

Read the Bible

Maybe you've seen the cartoon. In the first panel, a man is pleading for God to speak to him. The next panel shows a huge arm and hand reaching down from heaven to give the man a Bible.

It's funny because it's true.

We believe the Bible is the Word of God and that we hear from God when we read it. Earlier, we looked at 2 Timothy 3:16, which declares that the Bible is inspired by God. Let's look at that verse again, in the context of one additional verse: "All Scripture is inspired by God and is useful to teach us what is true and to make us realize what is wrong in our lives. It corrects us when we are wrong and teaches us to do what is right. *God uses it to prepare and equip his people to do every good work*" (2 Timothy 3:16-17, italics added).

Paul's words to his protégé Timothy make it clear: When we read the Bible, it teaches us to do what is right and to avoid what is wrong. But even more than that, reading the Bible *prepares* and *equips* us to do the works God has planned for us. (See also Ephesians 2:10.)

Read the Bible every day. It will help you stand firm in the faith (Ephesians 6:10–17).

Prioritize Prayer

Prayer might be the most talked about but least acted upon spiritual discipline of the Christian faith. We will look at the discipline of prayer in greater depth in chapter 6, but first we must understand that prayer is a critically important discipline for remaining strong in our faith.

When we read the Bible, we hear God's word directly. When we pray, we are in a conversation with God. Prayer is not merely a discipline; it is an honor of the highest magnitude. We are welcomed into the presence of the Creator and the King of kings.

There are hundreds of verses about prayer in the Bible. Paul, for example, says succinctly, "Devote yourselves to prayer with an alert mind and a thankful heart" (Colossians 4:2). The word *devote* carries the sense of being consumed with something. Prayer should be a burning desire for all believers. Prayer is powerful. Prayer is effective. Prayer leads us to grow more deeply in the things we believe.

Share What You Believe

My wife, Nellie Jo, is a consummate encourager. I have watched her lift the spirits of people who were totally discouraged. She simply has a positive word for anyone—friend or stranger—who crosses her path.

Several years ago, she discovered she could use her gift of exhortation and encouragement to be a gospel bearer. Simply stated, she realized that the greatest encouragement she could offer someone was Jesus.

She is totally unassuming in her gospel witness. She has prayed in public for people who are hurting. She has sat down for long conversations with acquaintances who are curious about the Christian faith.

Nellie Jo doesn't merely believe; she *shares* what she believes; she ties her beliefs to gospel action. This imperative will be unpacked more fully in chapter 5. It isn't enough merely to believe. We must be so convinced of our beliefs that we feel compelled to share them with others.

When Peter and John were jailed and faced long imprisonment or even death, they had an opportunity to walk away with no further punishment. There was just one stipulation: They could no longer speak in the name of Jesus.

Their response was swift, decisive, and powerful: "Do you think God wants us to obey you rather than him? We cannot stop telling about everything we have seen and heard" (Acts 4:19-20).

If you are a believer, you will grow stronger as you share your belief with others.

I am a believer.

I hope the beginning of this book has made it clear that, as Christians, we are compelled and commanded to live our lives in the company of other believers.

Yes, we are believers, but we are believers in the company of other Christians—which is called *the church*.

That is the subject of our next chapter.

DISCUSSION QUESTIONS

1. Imagine you are explaining to someone why beliefs are important to your faith. What would you say?

2. James says, "Just as the body is dead without breath, so also faith is dead without good works" (James 2:26). What does he mean by this? How does it relate to what you believe?

3. If someone asked you why reading the Bible is important, how would you respond?

2

I AM A CHURCH MEMBER

Do you remember the day you were born?

Of course you don't. It's a silly question.

But you know that on the day you were born, you were born into a family. Your family might have been healthy or unhealthy, fractured or fantastic, but you were born into it. You were not born in isolation.

We use the word *born* to describe when we leave our mother's womb and enter the world. Just as physical birth moves us from the darkness of the womb to the light of day, spiritual birth moves us from the darkness of sin to the light of Christ. Jesus used the phrase "born again" to describe our spiritual birth, which happens when we accept Jesus as our Lord and Savior. Look at John 3:3: "Jesus replied, 'I tell you the truth, unless you are born again, you cannot see the Kingdom of God.'"

In the previous chapter, we looked at the beautiful reality of becoming a believer. When we accepted Christ as our Savior, we became children of God.

But there's more. When we became Christians, when we were born again, we became part of a great family of believers. We call other Christians our brothers and sisters in Christ because we are in the same family.

THE UNIVERSAL CHURCH AND THE LOCAL CHURCH

When we are born again, we become members of the universal church, which includes all believers down through the ages. But our connection to the universal church is intended to be through a local congregation. We are not "born again" in isolation.

Indeed, the majority of New Testament books were written about, for, and to local churches. The book of Acts gives us a glimpse into the Holy Spirit's work in the churches of Jerusalem, Antioch, Cyprus, Antioch of Pisidia, Iconium, Lystra, Pamphylia, Macedonia, Thyatira, Thessalonica, Berea, Athens, Corinth, Caesarea, Ephesus, Troas, Rome, Malta, and other places along the way.

The apostle Paul wrote letters to specific local churches

or to leaders of local churches. These letters account for more than one-quarter of the New Testament: Romans, 1–2 Corinthians, Galatians, Ephesians, Philippians, Colossians, 1–2 Thessalonians, 1–2 Timothy, Titus, and Philemon. The final book of the Bible, Revelation, notes the spiritual condition of seven churches in Asia.

Do you get the picture? Local churches are important. Being a Christian outside the fellowship of a local church is not a biblical option.

THE JOURNEY TO GROW IN CHRIST . . . THROUGH THE CHURCH

Please read the next sentence carefully: *The New Testament does not have a plan for growing us as Christians outside of the local church.* From Acts 2 to Revelation 3, the New Testament is all about the local church. It leaves no doubt that God wants local congregations to be at the center of Christian ministry.

The Christian life is a journey of personal spiritual growth, but it is not one we undertake alone. It is a journey we take in the company of other believers. Sure, we practice some spiritual disciplines, such as prayer and Bible reading, on our own. But the assumption throughout the New Testament is that we will continuously and regularly gather with a local congregation for mutual service, growth, giving, and accountability.

Since Christian life is a journey in community, there is no such thing as an "inactive church member." There are no waysides where we "stop out" and let the others go on ahead. Growing in Christ means, essentially, growing in our commitment as church members. We are part of the body of Christ. We cannot separate our connection to the head, Jesus, from our connection to the rest of his body, the church. If we are fully committed to Christ, we will be fully committed to our local church. The moment our commitment to the local church begins to wane, our growth in Christ wanes as well.

TWO BAD PERCEPTIONS OF THE LOCAL CHURCH

Unfortunately, people do not always have the right perspective when they join a local church. Some church members act as if the church is a civic club. These members see the local church as a place to do good deeds for the community and have enjoyable meetings. When you give to a "civic club" church, you are paying your dues to help the church do its good deeds and underwrite its activities.

Even worse, other church members act like the church is a country club. They pay their dues and expect certain perks in return. These members want to tell the pastor what to preach and for how long. They want to dictate how the facilities look. They want the order of worship precisely as they prefer. They want their programs, their ministries, and their priorities.

Perhaps the worst aspect of the "country club" church is that members tend to see the pastors and staff as hired hands whose job is to meet their needs. After all, they're paying the bills.

But what happens when country club church members have contradictory preferences and demands? We typically call it a church fight. Left to fester, it can become a church split. It reminds me of a story I heard years ago about a congregational split where both new entities wanted to preserve their connection to the original church. Thus, one church became two: Harmony Church and Greater Harmony Church.

Instead of seeing our churches as civic clubs or country clubs, we need to get a clear New Testament view of the local church. This view is often dramatically different from the way we "do church" today. We will examine this view in the following sections.

I AM AN ATTENDING CHURCH MEMBER

Can you imagine standing at the wedding altar, vowing to love your spouse in every circumstance—except you may or may not come home on a given night? In fact, you might show up only once a month. After all, "attendance" at home is not all that important. Crazy, right?

One of the clearest commitments in a healthy marriage is to be present and accounted for with your spouse. Likewise, one of the clearest commitments in a healthy church is to be present and accounted for when the church gathers. This means giving church attendance priority over sleeping in, Sunday sports (kids and pro), days off, and a plethora of other excuses.

In our modern church history, a lot of people have decided that showing up at church is a low priority. Consequently, a church with two hundred members might have a weekly attendance of fifty.

That's not the way it's supposed to be.

When the first church started in Jerusalem, they began by meeting together: "All the believers met together in one place and shared everything they had. . . . They worshiped together at the Temple each day" (Acts 2:44, 46).

Every church to which Paul wrote a letter had a congregation that met together faithfully. They met in a specific city, often in the same location each week. They understood the importance of gathering as the body of Christ. They understood the importance of showing up.

When Paul wrote to the church at Corinth, he addressed a number of issues, one of which was the need for orderly worship. In fact, it was such a big issue that he devoted four full chapters to it (1 Corinthians 11–14). Paul obviously put a high priority on gathered worship if he saw the need to provide so much instruction on how it should be done.

Some people are fond of saying, "The church is not a building; it's the people." The implication is that we shouldn't focus on people gathering in a building. After all, we are the church wherever we go. That argument is a bit of a red herring. Whether the church meets under a tree, in a school, or in a traditional church building, the point is that we are supposed to gather. For certain, much of the New Testament is written to and about the gathered church. The writer of Hebrews speaks directly to the issue: "Let us hold tightly without wavering to the hope we affirm, for God can be trusted to keep his promise. Let us think of ways to motivate one another to acts of love and good works. And let us not neglect our meeting together, as some people do, but encourage one another, especially now that the day of his return is drawing near" (Hebrews 10:23-25).

We must meet together to hold on to the hope God has given us. We must meet together to motivate one another. We must meet together to encourage one another.

Church attendance is more important than all the excuses we can offer. I know committed church members who attend a church in person even when they are out of town or on vacation. Such a view might seem legalistic, but it's not. It's simply obedience to the mandate of Scripture. It is a commitment to put the good of others before our own. It is deciding that the body of Christ is not a part-time or occasional commitment. It's that important. Indeed, it is eternally important.

I AM A SERVING CHURCH MEMBER

My favorite biblical metaphor for the church is "the body of Christ" (1 Corinthians 12:12-13). On the one hand, the metaphor reminds us of the importance of the entire congregation: we are one body. On the other hand, we also see the importance of each individual part of the body. Without the parts, there would be no body.

By the way, we get the term *member* from the Bible's discussion of the church, not from the secular world of civic organizations or country clubs. A member, or part, is what is necessary to make the body whole. Paul explains this well in 1 Corinthians 12:25-26: "This makes for harmony among the members, so that all the members care for each other. If one part suffers, all the parts suffer with it, and if one part is honored, all the parts are glad."

The entirety of 1 Corinthians 12 is a beautiful picture of what a healthy church looks like. Paul takes the body metaphor deeper and explains that we should act as if we are one of many body parts:

Yes, the body has many different parts, not just one part. If the foot says, "I am not a part of the body

because I am not a hand," that does not make it any
less a part of the body. And if the ear says, "I am
not a part of the body because I am not an eye,"
would that make it any less a part of the body? If the
whole body were an eye, how would you hear? Or if
your whole body were an ear, how would you smell
anything?

1 CORINTHIANS 12:14-17

Let's unpack how this metaphor applies to you as a
church member. Your role is to serve, not to be served. Your
role is to minister, not to demand ministry for yourself.
Your role is to put others before yourself, not to seek to get
your own way.

When you became a believer in Christ, the mandate to
gather together, serve together, and minister together applied
to you immediately. Paul makes the point emphatically clear:
"All of you together are Christ's body, and each of you is a
part of it" (1 Corinthians 12:27).

When you become a part of a local church, your role is
to find places to serve. My first church had seven members
when I began serving as their pastor. The second person to
join our church after me was a man named Steve. I had the
opportunity to share the gospel with him, and he became a
follower of Christ.

Steve presented something of a challenge, however. I was

a new pastor with absolutely no training, and Steve was a new church member with absolutely no idea of what that entailed. We were both clueless.

Having been called to the pastorate from the business world, I was only in my second year of seminary. Steve was a good man, but he came from a rough, hard-drinking, coarse-talking background, and he had been visiting our church for only a few weeks before he became a Christian.

Steve asked me to meet him for breakfast one morning, where he explained that he didn't know what to do next as a new Christian. He especially didn't know what he was supposed to do next at church. Almost impulsively, I exclaimed, "Steve, you can be our greeter!"

Now, I have no idea why those words came out of my mouth. I know I was desperate to show Steve that I could guide him as his pastor. I often felt embarrassed when my inexperience showed, and in those moments my ego got in the way of common sense and humility.

Steve then asked the obvious question, "What does a greeter do?"

With only nine people total, we didn't have any type of welcome ministry, so I felt free to devise my own plan. In essence, I told Steve to stand in front of the church building about fifteen minutes before the Sunday morning service and welcome people to the church.

"Just be yourself," I told him naively.

The following Sunday, we had a young couple visit us for the first time. I could tell when they entered the building that they were a little confused, if not uncomfortable. I immediately moved toward them and introduced myself.

Then the bomb dropped.

"Well," the young man said, "I must say I've never been to a church where I've been greeted with a string of profanities."

I realized that Steve and I needed to have a time of training together.

Frankly, I spent a lot of time pointing out the cuss words in Steve's vocabulary. It was so ingrained that he didn't even know when he was cussing. And that led to another issue when Steve gave his testimony in church: He told the congregation that I had helped him a lot with his cuss words.

The story has a great ending, however. Steve not only became an incredible greeter, but he also served in our evangelistic ministry, in our men's ministry, and in our food and clothing ministry.

When you become a Christian and connect with a church, you are called to serve. Most churches have a number of ministries where you can get involved immediately. Don't just sit in a pew or chair. Don't wait to be served by others. Serve. Serve again. And serve with joy.

We will expand on this theme of service in chapter 4.

I AM A UNIFYING CHURCH MEMBER

Are you familiar with 1 Corinthians 13? We often call it "the love chapter." Paul penned the beautiful words that conclude with the crescendo, "Three things will last forever—faith, hope, and love—and the greatest of these is love" (1 Corinthians 13:13).

Perhaps you've heard 1 Corinthians 13 read at a wedding—after all, the love chapter seems to fit well with the theme of a wedding. And there's certainly nothing wrong with including these words in a wedding ceremony.

But the famous love chapter was written by Paul to address conflict and selfishness in the church at Corinth. The issues at hand were disorderly worship and confusion, but the church had a plethora of other problems: claims of spiritual superiority over one another, abuse of the communal meal in the church, sexual misconduct, and church members suing one another.

As Paul addressed each issue specifically, he wrote the thirteenth chapter to establish how church members should relate to one another. They must demonstrate love by putting others before themselves. Members can prophesy, but the prophecies are nothing if they're given without love. They may have great faith and be abundant givers, but it amounts to nothing without love. They can even sacrifice their lives in martyrdom, but it is to no avail without love.

Paul sent a resoundingly clear message: Demonstrate love and unity by putting others before yourselves.

Our team at Church Answers has dealt with hundreds of churches embroiled in conflict. The disagreements are rarely over doctrine or critical church issues. Instead, arguments are most often the result of some church members not getting their way or not having their personal preferences met.

Members might complain about the order of worship, the length of the pastor's sermon, the temperature in the sanctuary, or their preferred ministry not being mentioned in the announcements. The list of complaints can be very long.

But you have been called to be a unifying member of a church. You have been called to put yourself last instead of first.

The very first church, birthed in Jerusalem, was a church of unity. The description of this unity is explicit in the book of Acts: "All the believers were unified in heart and mind. And they felt that what they owned was not their own, so they shared everything they had" (Acts 4:32).

Paul, however, had to plead with the church at Corinth for unity: "I appeal to you, dear brothers and sisters, by the authority of our Lord Jesus Christ, to live in harmony with each other. Let there be no divisions in the church. Rather, be of one mind, united in thought and purpose" (1 Corinthians 1:10).

Yes, all Christians are expected to connect with a local church. But they should also be agents of unity and love. Unity and love occur supernaturally when we determine, in God's power, to put others before ourselves.

When we do, we imitate the greatest servant of all, Jesus.

I AM A GIVING MEMBER

Much debate about giving to the church is focused on what we are *required* to give rather than what we are *blessed* to give. Rather than being an act of joy, as God intended, giving often becomes a legalistic obligation. When Paul wrote to the church at Corinth, he commended them for their giving because it was an example to other churches and other believers: "In fact, it was your enthusiasm that stirred up many of the Macedonian believers to begin giving" (2 Corinthians 9:2).

Paul then summarizes the spiritual basis for giving:

> You must each decide in your heart how much
> to give. And don't give reluctantly or in response
> to pressure. "For God loves a person who gives
> cheerfully." And God will generously provide all
> you need. Then you will always have everything
> you need and plenty left over to share with others.
> 2 CORINTHIANS 9:7-8

As a word of personal testimony, one of the most financially liberating moments for me was when I finally understood that I have the joyous opportunity to give freely and generously rather than focusing on giving at a certain level. That freedom allowed Nellie Jo and me to look at the 10 percent tithe in the rearview mirror and give far more with great joy.

Giving to God's mission and his church is a gift and an opportunity—not something to be neglected.

I AM A PRAYING CHURCH MEMBER

Prayer is one of the most frequently mentioned—and misunderstood—words related to Christians. Prayer is often seen as just another activity or ministry of the church. But it is actually how God's Spirit accomplishes great works through the church.

Volumes have been written on prayer. More volumes could be written, and probably will be.

As church members, we should be people who pray. But what does that look like in our day-to-day lives and in the overall ministry of the church? Though I can't do justice to a full definition of prayer in a book of this size, I will give some practical examples in chapter 6. Stay tuned.

DISCUSSION QUESTIONS

1. If gathering with the local church, often called *church attendance*, is so important, why do you think so many church members fail to make it a priority?

2. Explain in a few sentences how 1 Corinthians 13, the love chapter, is really a chapter about healthy church membership.

3. Why do you think some church members struggle with the idea of giving?

I AM A DISCIPLE

What is the definition of discipleship? As Christians, we're told to "go and make disciples of all the nations" (Matthew 28:19), but what does that mean in practical terms?

We could peruse different dictionaries to define the term—and most of them get it pretty close. We are disciples when we follow a person, or when we follow a system promoted by that person. Discipleship is thus the process of helping people align themselves with the person or system they are following.

This raises the question: What process of discipleship should we use? More specifically for a follower of Jesus, how do we practically become more like Jesus? What steps do we take in our local churches to grow as disciples?

When I ask church leaders to describe their approach to discipleship, their responses are varied. Some tell me forthrightly they don't have a process or strategy for discipleship in their church. Others point to content or curriculum they provide for their members. Still others have a checklist of characteristics a disciple of Jesus must have.

Here is the reality if you are a Christian: You can say without hesitation, "I am a disciple." It is a settled reality. You have decided to follow Jesus. You have repented of your sins. You have trusted Christ and what he did for you on the cross to forgive your sins. You believe he rose from the dead and defeated death. You have decided to follow him through eternity.

But here is another reality: Until we get to heaven, we are supposed to grow as Christians. It is a process. Another way of saying this is that we are commanded to continue growing as fully devoted followers of Christ.

On February 23, 1980, the first of my three sons was born. At that very moment, I became a dad—by definition—and I could have concluded I had nothing left to do. But I wanted to be a *good* dad; I wanted to *grow* as a dad. I wanted to love my sons more deeply. When I made one of my countless mistakes as a dad, it deepened my resolve to do better.

I wasn't content to simply have the title of *Dad*. I wanted to be the best dad I could be.

The same thing applies to the title of *Christian*. I must

seek to become a better Christian. To put it another way, I must seek to become more like Christ.

I am a Christian is more than religious jargon. Those four words have profound implications. Let's look at some of them.

LOVE: THE GREATEST OF THESE (AGAIN)

In the previous chapter, we learned that "three things will last forever—faith, hope, and love—and the greatest of these is love" (1 Corinthians 13:13). Our examination of that verse focused on how we love in the context of the local church. But the love of God obviously has much broader implications.

We must begin with a basic premise: God is love. He does not merely *show* love; he *is* love in his very essence: "But anyone who does not love does not know God, for God is love" (1 John 4:8). God demonstrated his perfect love by sending his Son, Jesus, to die for us "while we were still sinners" (Romans 5:8).

When we seek to become more like Christ, our definition of discipleship must include that we love like Christ. While we cannot attain his perfect love, we can, through the power of the Holy Spirit at work in our lives, learn to increasingly love like he loves.

When Paul wrote to the church at Philippi, he commanded

them to be more like Christ. In other words, he told them to become more devoted disciples. In Philippians 2:2-4, Paul writes, "Make me truly happy by agreeing wholeheartedly with each other, loving one another, and working together with one mind and purpose. Don't be selfish; don't try to impress others. Be humble, thinking of others as better than yourselves. Don't look out only for your own interests, but take an interest in others, too."

What is Paul saying? If we are in unity with other Christians, if we are selfless, if we are humble, then we are becoming more like Christ. Indeed, we are demonstrating love like Christ's love. Paul sums up these traits in Philippians 2:5: "You must have the same attitude that Christ Jesus had."

When I look at these characteristics, I wonder if I can even come close to becoming that type of person. Then Paul powerfully reminds us: "For God is working in you, giving you the desire and the power to do what pleases him" (Philippians 2:13).

That verse has been a game changer for me. God not only gives us the power to become more like Christ, but he gives us the desire as well. My prayer life now includes expressing my desire to yield to God's power, knowing that God will give me the power to do things that make me more like Christ. Above all, he leads me to love others more, to put others before myself. And he gives me the desire to do it all with joy.

Such is the heart of discipleship.

LOVING THOSE WHO ARE NOT CHRISTIANS

Jesus had his critics. There were some religious leaders who did not like his association with sinners: "The Pharisees and their teachers of religious law complained bitterly to Jesus' disciples, 'Why do you eat and drink with such scum?'" (Luke 5:30).

Pretty harsh words.

Jesus was quick to respond: "Healthy people don't need a doctor—sick people do. I have come to call not those who think they are righteous, but those who know they are sinners and need to repent" (Luke 5:31-32).

Here we learn two important lessons about the love of Jesus, the love we are supposed to emulate. First, if the perfect man, the one who is God himself, chooses to associate with those deemed undesirable by the religious elite, should we not also associate with them? Jesus, who is perfect, made a point to eat and drink with people whom others viewed as scum. We who are forgiven sinners must follow that example. Some of our harshest critics might be those who are Christians in name only.

That brings us to our second important lesson: We must be ready and eager to associate with—and to share the gospel with—those who do not know Christ. Jesus used the metaphor of a doctor coming to heal sick people. The sickness, of course, is spiritual rather than physical.

The greatest act of love was an act of evangelism: God sent his only Son to be sacrificed. We who follow Jesus must be willing and eager to demonstrate and tell others about that love.

We can't truly call ourselves disciples of Jesus unless we love people so much that we can't stop telling people "everything we have seen and heard" (Acts 4:20) about the Savior and Lord we follow.

STAYING IN THE WORD

Several years ago, Brad Waggoner wrote a foundational book on discipleship called *The Shape of Faith to Come*. After examining the spiritual disciplines of 2,500 churchgoers, Waggoner discovered a consistent theme: Christians who read their Bibles daily were more likely to grow in all areas of their spiritual development.

They were more likely to obey God.

They were more likely to share their faith.

They were more likely to serve others.

They were more likely to learn deeper truths about the Christian faith.

It makes sense, doesn't it? When you read the Bible, you are reading God's Word. You are hearing from God. You are finding out what his plan is for your life.

A pastor from Arizona recently told me that if he could

get his church members to do only one thing, he would get them to read the Bible every day. Two years earlier, his church had had a major campaign where most active members committed to read their Bibles every day for six months. The pastor said that the change in many of the members was "a stunning transformation."

Do you really want to grow as a Christian? Do you really want to be more like Christ? Read your Bible. Study your Bible. Read it in your quiet time. Study with others in a group. Be a consistent and daily reader of Scripture. Whether you try to read the entire Bible in a year or do a deep dive on a particular book or section of the Bible, read it every day.

Start or join a small group in your church and study the Bible with them. I am always amazed at the insights my community group members provide. We should all love to study in community.

Though it sounds obvious, study the Bible as your pastor preaches. Open your Bible to the sermon text. Follow along with the teaching. Read the Bible carefully as your pastor teaches the different verses.

It's simple but profound: We can't become more like Jesus until we know more about Jesus. And the Bible is where we learn about our Savior from his pre-incarnate days of the Old Testament to his incarnation to his ascension and future return.

I am a Christian.

Do you really want those words to mean something for you?

Read your Bible. It's life-changing.

THE CHALLENGE OF FORGIVENESS

When you think about Jesus, what are the first thoughts that come to mind? I think of his death on the cross. In a given day, it's not unusual for me to think several times about Jesus on the cross.

When the thought comes to mind, I am often stirred. He *died* for me. And he didn't just die; he died an agonizing death on a Roman cross, one of the cruelest forms of death imaginable.

It's hard for me to fully comprehend this truth.

He died an excruciating death for me. Why? Because he loves me. Because he was taking the punishment for my sin. He died so that God could forgive me.

I don't deserve his love. I don't deserve his forgiveness. But he died for me anyway.

How, then, do I respond as one of his disciples? Paul's instructions are unequivocal: "Get rid of all bitterness, rage, anger, harsh words, and slander, as well as all types of evil behavior. Instead, be kind to each other, tenderhearted, forgiving one another, just as God through Christ has forgiven you" (Ephesians 4:31-32).

Jesus also delivered a crystal-clear message about forgiveness. Look at his response when "Peter came to him and asked, 'Lord, how often should I forgive someone who sins against me? Seven times?'

"'No, not seven times,' Jesus replied, 'but seventy times seven!'" (Matthew 18:21-22).

The difficulty and necessity of forgiveness became real to me after I was physically abused by one of my teachers in high school. He was angry that I wouldn't play on the team he coached. Though he never touched me directly, he took me behind the school and had some of his players beat me to a pulp. This happened more than once over the course of several weeks.

I became an angry and bitter person. I hated him. I would not forgive him. For years, I carried the burden of an unforgiving spirit.

Fourteen years after the abuse ended, I was called to pastor my first church. In the first week of my tenure, as I tried to prepare my very first sermon, the image of this teacher kept coming to my mind. I knew what I had to do.

For the first time in my life, I prayed and forgave that man. Though I never saw him after high school, I prayed to forgive him as if he were standing right in front of me. No, I didn't experience a miraculous wave of love for him, but God gradually removed the bitterness from my heart. Indeed, I can write these words with objectivity many years later.

There were certainly aftereffects, even after I forgave him.

I still deal with anger issues. I still remember the abuse with some pain. But I truly forgave him over three decades ago, and I don't harbor any ill will toward him.

The text in Scripture that convicted me the most was Matthew 6:12, part of the passage we call "the Lord's Prayer," where Jesus is teaching his disciples how to pray. Regarding forgiveness, he says, "Forgive us our sins, as we have forgiven those who sin against us."

Jesus knew that forgiveness would be an issue for his disciples (including us), so he expanded his teaching on the issue: "If you forgive those who sin against you, your heavenly Father will forgive you. But if you refuse to forgive others, your Father will not forgive your sins" (Matthew 6:14-15).

Wow. Those words hit me just as hard today as they did thirty years ago. I knew I could not lead my new church if I didn't forgive my high school teacher. Even more, I knew I could not live as a committed disciple of Christ if I didn't forgive that man.

It's sometimes difficult to be a disciple. No, it is *always impossible* to be a disciple unless the Holy Spirit empowers us. Hold on to these words: "For God is working in you, giving you the desire and the power to do what pleases him" (Philippians 2:13).

Remember, God will give you both the desire and the power.

That is how you are able to be a disciple.

FORGIVE YOUR FELLOW CHURCH MEMBERS

There is a simple intersection between the topic of forgiveness and what it means to be a church member. The forgiveness we extend to others must include forgiveness for our fellow church members.

My team at Church Answers deals with a lot of hurt in churches. Members hurting each other. Members hurting pastors and staff. Pastors and staff hurting members. Pastors and staff hurting each other.

It is sad whenever a church becomes a place where fights ensue, harsh words are exchanged, and people come to resent each other. It's sad, but all too common. The Bible doesn't sugarcoat the problems that churches have. Read 1 or 2 Corinthians. Read Galatians.

If we are to grow as disciples, we must forgive other people. And that includes the people in the churches we serve.

Churches are messy. Churches are filled with hypocrites. But God, in his infinite wisdom, decided he would make the local church the primary vehicle for his mission. It is his plan A, and he doesn't have a plan B.

I am a Christian.
I am a church member.
I am a disciple.
I will forgive others.

In God's power, I will forgive others in my church. Because forgiveness is an absolute requirement to grow as a disciple.

I AM A DISCIPLE . . . AND SO MUCH MORE

No doubt you can tell by now that the chapters in this book are not stand-alones. They intersect at point after point.

There is so much more we could say about what it means to be a disciple. This chapter can only skim the surface.

We have examined some basic traits or characteristics of disciples—including love, forgiveness, Bible study, giving, prayer, and evangelism. The list can seem so lengthy at times that it begins to look like, well, a list. We may start to think that if we do this one and that one—if we check off all the items—then we have done our duty as Christians. In fact, we can become legalistic about it—especially toward others.

In the first century, Jesus pointed out a group of people who were list keepers and proud of it. They were called Pharisees. The Pharisees were proud because they were scrupulous keepers of the religious laws. They wore masks of righteousness to hide the hardness of heart and wickedness inside them.

Jesus had no patience for their hypocrisy. He went straight to the heart of the matter:

> What sorrow awaits you teachers of religious law
> and you Pharisees. Hypocrites! For you are like
> whitewashed tombs—beautiful on the outside but
> filled on the inside with dead people's bones and all
> sorts of impurity. Outwardly you look like righteous
> people, but inwardly your hearts are filled with
> hypocrisy and lawlessness.
>
> MATTHEW 23:27-28

In many ways, I take comfort that Jesus didn't bless the Pharisees or look the other way, but instead chose to associate with the lawbreakers, tax collectors, rebels, and prostitutes: the broken and the downcast. Deep inside, I identify more closely with them. They were sinners, and they knew it. They were sinners, and they sought forgiveness. They were sinners and were given chance after chance after chance. What did Jesus say? We must forgive seventy times seven.

My sons have several of Nellie Jo's and my traits. While they were growing up in our home, they didn't take copious notes about our behaviors and actions and try to emulate them in checklist fashion. They simply watched us and learned from us, the good and the bad.

As we seek to understand more fully what it means to be a Christian, remember that we are not looking to check items off a list. We are seeking to be like Jesus. My prayer for you is that you will simply observe Jesus' life, and in his power, seek to be like him. The checklist traits will follow naturally as you draw closer to Christ.

DISCUSSION QUESTIONS

1. What are some key ways for you to stay in the Bible every day?

2. Why is evangelism one of the best ways we can say we love the world?

3. A longtime, mature believer told me that forgiving those who hurt him deeply was a faith challenge. Have you ever been hurt deeply by someone? Did you forgive him or her? How did you do it?

4

I AM A SERVANT

Meet Jess Keller.

He is with Jesus now, but I still want you to meet him.

He's my uncle and one of my heroes of the faith. He was one of those Christians who demonstrated servanthood every day I knew him.

I always admired Jess, but we became especially close after my dad died. Jess immediately began serving me at that critical point in my life. He knew he could not replace my dad, but he wanted to be there for me as much as possible.

It was not like Jess had a lot of time on his hands. He was a prominent attorney with more business than he could handle. He was smart, but also wise. He was savvy, but also service oriented.

Jess and I communicated every week. We had a bond that was unique and a mutual love that was unmistakable.

I didn't realize the full depth and breadth of his servant-hood until after he died. I guess I had always focused on our relationship, not realizing how he served countless others as well. I preached his funeral sermon, but my awakening to my uncle's God-given servanthood came after the funeral.

Many people wanted to tell me what Jess had done for them. One couple told me with tears that Jess had saved their marriage. They told me he spent hours with them, speaking truth in love, both encouraging and admonishing them.

A local businessman shared with me that he had gone to Jess ready to declare bankruptcy. My uncle worked with him on ways to save his business—and never charged him any legal fees.

An elderly woman told me about a strong storm that knocked down a tree in her yard. Jess had immediately organized a crew with saws to remove the tree and other debris. The men were in her yard as soon as the storm abated.

The stories seemed endless, and I was astounded. I had no idea he served so many people.

Nellie Jo and I named our first two sons after their grandfathers. Sam was named for my dad, and Art was named for Nellie Jo's dad. When our third son was born, we knew we had another "grandfather" ready for a namesake. We named our third son Jess.

I have tears in my eyes even today, knowing that my son is named after a man I loved so dearly. Uncle Jess embodied servanthood more than anyone I know.

SERVANTS AND SLAVES

In the New Testament, the Greek word *doulos* is translated as either *servant* or *slave*, depending on the Bible translation you're using.

It's easy to see the challenge in translating this word. *Servant* is often the preferred alternative to *slave* because of the image of bondage, cruelty, and suffering associated with slavery in world history. Translators are hesitant to use a word so closely associated with oppression. Some will point out that "slavery" in the first century was often *indentured service*, with the possibility of earning one's freedom. But I'm sure it was no picnic, even under the best of circumstances.

The word *servant* may not adequately communicate the depth of the meaning of *doulos*. Though human history has been marred with the blight of involuntary slavery, those who become a *doulos* to Christ take on that role freely and with joy. They choose to come under the ownership of a master who is totally loving and giving. Slaves to Christ are not coerced. Far from it. Rather, we are compelled by joy to freely and fully submit ourselves to him.

Our Master, Jesus Christ, purchased us with the high

price of his own life (1 Corinthians 6:20). We who have become slaves to Jesus have chosen to abandon our own lives and rights in order to serve our King faithfully and joyfully.

What, then, are some implications of declaring, "I am a servant"? Here are a few to consider.

FREELY CHOOSING TO BE LAST

My family loves to vacation at a beach in Florida that is one of the few remote places remaining in the state. It has few amenities, but one of them is a donut shop. For some reason, the owner never makes enough donuts to meet demand. He always sells out early.

The line outside the donut shop forms early each morning. Some people wait more than an hour to get their donut fix. And don't even think about cutting in line. Those who have already secured their spots will let you know the consequences of such foolishness in no uncertain terms.

And that's just for a bag of donuts. The first shall be first.

The mindset of the servant is just the opposite. Being a servant is not just choosing to be last; it is desiring to be last. A servant mindset is totally counterintuitive in our culture today.

In the Bible, the twelve disciples learned this lesson when the mother of James and John made an unthinkable request of Jesus. Her sons were already close followers of Jesus, but she wanted them to be even closer. Read her request to Jesus carefully: "In your Kingdom, please let my two sons sit in places of honor next to you, one on your right and the other on your left" (Matthew 20:21).

The seats next to a king are not only seats of honor, but also seats of power. The mother of James and John made a totally unreasonable request. And when the other disciples heard about it, they were not happy: "When the ten other disciples heard what James and John had asked, they were indignant" (Matthew 20:24).

Jesus quelled the tension. He called together all the disciples and explained what they were missing: "You know that the rulers in this world lord it over their people, and officials flaunt their authority over those under them" (Matthew 20:25).

I wonder whether Jesus paused for a moment after this sentence. I wonder if he let his disciples absorb those words before he told them they must take a different path.

"But among you it will be different. Whoever wants to be a leader among you must be your servant, and whoever wants to be first among you must become your slave. For even the Son of Man came not to be served but to serve others and to give his life as a ransom for many" (Matthew 20:26-28).

And there it is.

Do you want to be like Jesus? Serve others.

Do you want to be like Jesus? Choose to be last.

Do you want to be like Jesus? Be willing to sacrifice your life.

This passage in the Bible is one where I would love to have more details. Did the disciples get it? Did they stay mad at James and John? Did they repent of their attitude? Did they commit to the new reality that being a follower of Christ meant being a servant both to him and to others?

"Those who are last now will be first then, and those who are first will be last" (Matthew 20:16).

God placed you in a local church to live out your servant-hood to Jesus. He put you in the congregation where you are now so that you can put others first.

Regardless of the words or actions of other church members, *you* can choose to be a servant. Be willing to set aside your preferences and desires for the preferences and desires of others.

Choosing to become a servant in my church has been a truly liberating decision. I don't have to scheme and fight to get my own way. I don't have to push to the front of the line. I don't have to demand my rights.

I remember witnessing an example of servanthood in an airport when a flight I was scheduled to take was canceled. Passengers were angry. The line at the counter to rebook flights was growing. Many decided to take out their frustration on the agent at the desk. That is, until the lady in front of me in line spoke gently to the woman.

"I know the cancellation is not your fault. I know you're doing all you can to help us. Please know that I am praying for you as you work through this mess."

She then said a brief prayer before concluding with these words: "I will step to the back of the line so you can serve the others."

There I was. The lady stepped away, and I was staring into the face of the booking agent, who now had tears in her eyes.

"She's right," I said. "You are doing everything you can."

Then I left to go to the end of the line, where once again I was standing behind the lady who had spoken kindly to the agent. I tapped her on the shoulder.

"Excuse me," I said. "I hope you don't mind my asking, but are you a Christian?"

She paused, perhaps taken aback by my question.

"Yes," she said. "How did you know?"

I smiled. She was a servant, that's how.

SEEKING TO PLEASE THE MASTER

A true servant wants to please his or her master. A true servant will do whatever it takes to follow both the teachings and commands of the master.

Do you remember when the acronym WWJD was popular in the 1990s? It meant, "What would Jesus do?" It was the theme of a book called *In His Steps*, written in 1896 by Charles

Sheldon. With more than 50 million copies sold, this is one of the bestselling books of all time. It obviously struck a chord.

Without giving away the entire plot of the book, I will provide a brief introduction. A homeless man walks into a church service and challenges the congregation. He calmly tells them that he has seen no evidence of the work of God by the church in the community. He essentially confronts them to ask if their faith is real.

After speaking, the homeless man collapses. He dies a few days later.

That incident shakes some church members' foundations of faith. The church members begin to make decisions by asking, "What would Jesus do?" The book essentially captures what would happen if Christians were to actually live out their faith.

It's not uncommon to hear people at church say that they have accepted Jesus as Lord and Savior. The latter title, Savior, is pretty easy to proclaim. After all, Jesus saved us from our sins. Jesus saved us from condemnation. Jesus saved us for eternal life.

But do we truly grasp the meaning of the title *Lord*?

It certainly means we confess that Jesus is God. He is the one true God. There are no other gods.

Acknowledging Jesus as Lord also means that we recognize that he has all authority. It is his Kingdom, and he reigns over all creation and eternity.

Confessing Jesus as Lord also defines the posture of our

relationship to him. To say that Jesus is our Lord means that we willingly subject ourselves to his authority. We want to please him.

Jesus clearly challenged those who would take his lordship lightly: "Why do you keep calling me 'Lord, Lord!' when you don't do what I say? I will show you what it's like when someone comes to me, listens to my teaching, and then follows it" (Luke 6:46-47).

We cannot be servants of Jesus unless we submit to his authority and follow him as our Lord. Calling him *Lord* means surrendering to him as our master. We strive to live for him. We seek to answer the question, "What would Jesus do?" in all our actions and thoughts.

LOVING OTHERS BY SERVING OTHERS

We have clearly seen that our Christian faith requires us to demonstrate love. The love we show should first be to Christ and then to others. We can show our love for others in countless ways, but one of the most obvious is by serving.

In John 13, Jesus does something that astounds his disciples. He wraps a towel around his waist, pours water into a basin, and begins washing the disciples' feet one by one. That is, until he comes to Simon Peter. In keeping with his impetuous temperament, Peter objects: "Lord, are you going to wash my feet?" (John 13:6).

Jesus calmly responds, "You don't understand now what I am doing, but someday you will" (John 13:7).

When Peter still objects, Jesus does not mince words: "Unless I wash you, you won't belong to me" (John 13:8).

Foot washing was dirty work, usually delegated to a house servant. Most people wore sandals on their feet, which provided some protection but didn't keep their feet from getting dirty on dusty roads and paths.

It was the lowliest of tasks. It was likely very unpleasant. But it is an example of what it means to love other people by serving them.

After Jesus washed the disciples' feet, he said, "Since I, your Lord and Teacher, have washed your feet, you ought to wash each other's feet" (John 13:14).

There it is: Not even the lowliest of tasks will be beneath us when we seek to serve our Lord by serving others.

I am a Christian means *I am a servant.*

SERVING WITH OUR TREASURES

I was once a twenty-something young businessman trying to figure out the meaning of discipleship. Though I became a Christian as a teenager, I did not start growing as a believer until my wife told me she was pregnant with our first child. That, without a doubt, was a wake-up call for me.

The thought of becoming a dad both exhilarated and

terrified me. I couldn't wait for my son to come into this world, but I was clueless about parenthood. There was one thing I knew for certain: I would have to depend on God completely if I was to be the kind of dad I needed to be.

My wife and I joined a church. She had been gently pushing me in this direction, but I no longer needed a push. I was ready.

One of the most pivotal events for me was joining a men's Bible study. Even to this day, decades later, I remember all the men in that group by name. I loved being in the class. I thrived in that setting.

I was growing each week as we studied the Bible, and I guess I thought that was all I had to do. But one day, in the middle of December, the leader, Chris, spoke up and said we needed to do more than simply study the Word. We also needed to *live* the Word, to do what it said. I wasn't sure where he was going with this idea, but he explained it at our next meeting.

"All right, men," he began. "Let's do something to show we really love others. I have become aware of a young single mom in our area who has some challenges. She works two jobs, lives in a dilapidated mobile home, and has no money to buy her three young kids Christmas gifts. It's time for us to do something to serve someone."

Chris divided our class into three groups of four. The first group was the home repair group. Several items in the young woman's home were in dire need of repair. Knowingly or not, Chris wisely didn't put me in this group. Given my total inability to fix anything, that was a good decision.

Instead, he put me in charge of the finance group. My role was to raise money for gifts, food, and supplies. I did a decent job of collecting funds from my fellow group members and a few others. But then I became convicted that I should give the largest amount, in essence matching what everyone else had given.

With my wife's blessing, I withdrew cash from our bank account, the largest amount I had ever given. I wondered whether I was making a big mistake with our limited funds. But any second thoughts quickly evaporated a few days later.

With the young mom's permission, the fix-it group made repairs on her home while she was at work. And they didn't stop with the list she had given them. They also landscaped her small yard, finishing it off with a little picket fence.

Others went shopping for both the mom and her children. We asked for a Christmas gift list, but we had to return to the mother and ask her to add to it. Her list was too modest. We wanted to do more.

When we were done, we waited for her to arrive home from work. When she pulled up in her car with the three kids, I could see the stunned look on her face. Tears flowed.

She could not believe how her home looked from the outside. Then she went inside to see the work the men had done in there. Three appliances had been replaced with brand-new ones. The old, worn carpet had been replaced as well. The cabinets were repaired and repainted. Those are just a few of the repairs and additions our men's group had made.

Though she didn't have a Christmas tree when we arrived, now there was a fully decorated tree in the corner of the living room, with an abundance of gifts underneath for all four family members.

As we left, I presented her with the cash we had left over after making all the purchases. I will never forget the look on her face—it was one of joy and hope.

I learned something very important from that men's Bible study group. We can serve others in many ways, including giving abundantly. Jesus' teaching on this topic is powerful:

> Don't store up treasures here on earth, where moths
> eat them and rust destroys them, and where thieves
> break in and steal. Store your treasures in heaven,
> where moths and rust cannot destroy, and thieves
> do not break in and steal. Wherever your treasure is,
> there the desires of your heart will also be.
>
> MATTHEW 6:19-21

Serving by giving is an investment in eternity.

WAITING EXPECTANTLY FOR OUR MASTER

One of my favorite online video genres is the unexpected reunion of a spouse or children with a loved one who has served overseas in the military. The moment when the child or spouse realizes who is right there in front of them is both classic and emotional.

I can only watch one a day lest I expend all my emotions on video posts. But I love that moment of reunion.

Being a Christian means waiting expectantly for our Lord's return.

One day we will see Jesus face-to-face. Either we will die and meet him in heaven, or he will return to get us. Either way, we will see him in person.

As Christians, we look forward to that reunion with great anticipation. We are servants awaiting the return of our loving master. Though we wait expectantly, that moment will far exceed the greatest expectations we have.

As servants, we serve Christ and others with joy on this side of heaven. But we also anticipate an incredible reunion with our Lord and Savior when we enter eternity. We get both the joy of serving Jesus in the present and the joy of meeting him face-to-face in the days to come.

The parable of the talents in Matthew 25 is a grand picture of a servant who serves the master faithfully. When the faithful servant is called to give an account of his service,

Jesus exudes with praise: "Well done, my good and faithful servant" (Matthew 25:21).

So we wait.

We wait with eagerness and expectation.

We wait to see him face-to-face.

We wait with the promise that if we have served well, he will embrace us as good and faithful servants.

I am a Christian.

I am a servant.

I wait for my master's return.

DISCUSSION QUESTIONS

1. What do you see as the most biblically accurate understanding of the word *doulos*? Is it best translated as *servant* or *slave*? Why?

2. How can you demonstrate servanthood in your church this week?

3. Why is it important for a servant to wait expectantly for the master's return?

5

I AM A WITNESS

Have you ever watched a movie or television show in which an attorney reads a last will and testament to a group of relatives or friends? They all sit around nervously, waiting to hear whether they will receive riches or have been shunned by the deceased.

It's a pretty dramatic scene. As each beneficiary is named, you watch his or her reaction to the will. They might be celebrating newfound wealth or be in total shock to learn they have inherited only the sickly, fourteen-year-old dog. And after the attorney reads the final sentence of the will, there may be a few people in the room whose names were never mentioned. They sit in stunned silence or explode in selfish rage.

It is common in most of these scenes for one or more parties to threaten a lawsuit. If the show is a murder mystery, some beneficiaries may meet an untimely demise.

I have dealt with a few wills in my lifetime, both as a beneficiary and as an executor. Frankly, I've never witnessed the melodrama portrayed in movies or television shows. Sure, I've seen some people not handle the consequences of a last will and testament well. But I've never seen anyone be murdered or become a murderer.

I do know one thing about last wills and testaments. If they are done well and with forethought, they represent the heart and desires of the deceased. In many ways, they tell the story of what was important in the person's life. A common definition of *testament* is "an expression of conviction." As a life passes, these words reflect what was really on the heart of the deceased while he or she was still alive.

Jesus left us a last will and testament. He had already died on the cross. He had already been resurrected from the dead. And right before he ascended to heaven, he left his followers a few sets of instructions. They were among his last words on earth.

They were important words. We should heed them carefully.

One of the most widely known of these instructions is the Great Commission. We call it *great* because of the importance of the message. We call it a *commission* because it represents marching orders for Christians down through the ages, including you and me.

Matthew's account of the Great Commission is the most often cited:

> Jesus came and told his disciples, "I have been given all authority in heaven and on earth. Therefore, go and make disciples of all the nations, baptizing them in the name of the Father and the Son and the Holy Spirit. Teach these new disciples to obey all the commands I have given you. And be sure of this: I am with you always, even to the end of the age."
> MATTHEW 28:18-20

We are commissioned to go and share the gospel. We will then see the work of the Holy Spirit as people become disciples. We are to baptize and teach these disciples. And as we go and share in the authority of Christ, he will be with us every step of the way.

Don't lose sight of two very important issues related to the Great Commission. First, it is a *commandment*, something Jesus explicitly told his disciples to do. Second, it is a commandment *given to his disciples*. Those who were present when he spoke the words were to obey. And because the Holy Spirit inspired these words for future readers of Scripture, it is also a commandment for all followers of Jesus until he returns.

The Great Commission was for them. The Great Commission is for me. The Great Commission is for you.

Simply stated, we are commanded by Jesus to share the gospel with others.

Acts 1:8 is a powerful reminder of how important it is for us to be witnesses for Christ:

> You will receive power when the Holy Spirit comes
> upon you. And you will be my witnesses, telling people
> about me everywhere—in Jerusalem, throughout
> Judea, in Samaria, and to the ends of the earth.

There is no hesitancy in Jesus' words. They do not lack clarity. We *will* be his witnesses. As Christians, we are not given an option.

Don't miss the verse that follows: "After saying this, [Jesus] was taken up into a cloud while they were watching, and they could no longer see him" (Acts 1:9).

Acts 1:8 captures Jesus' last words before he ascended into heaven. They were his last will and testament.

That's how important it is to be his witnesses.

WHY IT IS IMPORTANT

I wonder how many times I said these words to my sons when they were young: "Because I said so, that's why." My exasperated reply was typically in response to an endless series of *whys*.

"Why do I have to brush my teeth?"

"Why do I have to go to bed?"

"Why do I have to wash my hands?"

"Why do I have to stop cutting my brother's hair?"

(Yes, these are all actual questions from my sons a few decades ago.)

Little children always want to know why, but Jesus left no doubt about why we should be his witnesses. Indeed, his reason is so powerful, it should go unquestioned.

At the Last Supper, Jesus had gathered his disciples one last time before he went to the cross. He wanted to make sure they understood what was about to happen. He told them he was leaving soon, but they obviously did not understand that he was going to heaven. He not only wanted them to know where he was going, but he also wanted them to understand how they (and others) could join him there.

He began by telling them not to worry about their eternal home:

Don't let your hearts be troubled. Trust in God, and trust also in me. There is more than enough room in my Father's home. If this were not so, would I have told you that I am going to prepare a place for you?
JOHN 14:1-2

Jesus was obviously referring to heaven, where he would be waiting for them. He added that he would be preparing heaven for them and he would return for them:

> When everything is ready, I will come and get you, so that you will always be with me where I am. And you know the way to where I am going.
> JOHN 14:3-4

But at least one of the disciples pleaded for clarity:

> "No, we don't know, Lord," Thomas said. "We have no idea where you are going, so how can we know the way?"
> JOHN 14:5

We don't know whether Thomas was speaking for himself, or if he had heard similar questions from the other disciples. In either case, Jesus responds with powerful clarity: "I am the way, the truth, and the life. No one can come to the Father except through me" (John 14:6).

Though you may be familiar with John 14:6, let the words soak in for a moment. There is no equivocation. There is no reservation. Jesus speaks clearly and decisively. He is the *only* way of salvation. He is the *only* way to heaven. No one goes to heaven except through faith in Jesus.

The theological word for this assertion is *exclusivism*. The way to heaven is narrow and absolute. It is only through Jesus.

Do you understand why it is so important to be a witness, to share the good news about Jesus? He is the only way of salvation. There are no escape clauses. No back doors. He is the way.

Thus, Jesus answers the "Why?" question with clarity and conviction. He is the only way of salvation. Others must be told that he is the only way of salvation. We who are believers have been chosen and mandated to tell others about Jesus. We are to be his witnesses.

Do you understand the urgency of the command? We should respond to every opportunity to share the gospel. We should be telling others the story of our own salvation. We must be witnesses.

On several occasions, I have told the story about how my high school football coach, Joe Hendrickson, shared the gospel with me. He simply asked me to meet him in his office so he could talk with me. He told me that Jesus was the only way of salvation. He told me how I could repent of my sins and place my faith in Christ. He challenged me to do so.

Later that night, I prayerfully committed myself to Christ. Though I don't recall the precise words I prayed, I knew I was a sinner who had to confess and repent of my sins. I knew I had to believe that Jesus died on the cross to take the punishment for me. And I knew he conquered death when he rose from the grave.

Coach Joe was a witness to me. He wanted me to have the opportunity to accept Christ as my only way of salvation.

So I did. As a teenage boy, I accepted Christ as the only way of salvation. And I knew I must be a witness of that truth to others.

WHEN YOU DON'T THINK YOU CAN

I wish I could say that my life is a daily stream of witnessing for Christ. The best I can say is that I am inconsistent. I get my priorities mixed up too often.

But I no longer say, "I can't." Saying "I can't" implies that I have neither the opportunity nor the ability to be a witness. I have learned differently.

When Jesus gave his disciples the Great Commission, he said, "I have been given all authority in heaven and on earth" (Matthew 28:18). So when we witness, we're not depending on our own knowledge or authority; we have been given the authority of the King of kings.

Jesus also said, "Be sure of this: I am with you always, even to the end of the age" (Matthew 28:20). When we witness on his behalf, we are not alone. To the contrary, Jesus is right there with us. He is both our authority and our power. So *can't* is simply not part of the equation. *Won't*? Maybe. *Can't*? Never.

To be clear, God gives you *everything* you need to be a witness for Christ. You don't need human eloquence or human-centered courage. As you share the gospel, continually rely on Jesus to be with you and to empower you. He will answer that prayer every time with a resounding yes.

TWO MAJOR STEPS TO BECOMING A WITNESS

When we witness for Christ, we obviously are witnessing to *someone*. How, then, do we find people who are willing to listen? What are some practical steps we can follow?

First, we must develop relationships. Those "relationships" might be very brief, such as during an airplane ride or while getting a haircut, or longstanding, such as with a friend or coworker. But we must begin by *connecting* with the various people we encounter in our daily lives.

Even with brief encounters, there is often the potential for a new and longer relationship. You could choose to have the same stylist cut your hair. You could find a service person you call on regularly. For example, Jason has been mowing my yard for years. He is not yet a believer, but I still pray for God to give me opportunities to share with him. Matt does handyman work for me. I've had the opportunity to speak with him on many occasions.

Second, your relationship with an unbeliever must, at some point, evolve into a gospel conversation. You might have the opportunity to share how you became a Christian. When we ask God to provide those opportunities, we must be sensitive to the leading of the Holy Spirit and his timing for us to speak.

I believe that God will give us all the opportunities our obedience will allow. We must be willing to take those opportunities. We must be sensitive to the Holy Spirit to know when to speak. And we must believe courageously that the Spirit will give us the right words at the right time.

My prayer for all of us is that we will be unable to stop speaking about Jesus to others.

THE SIMPLE ACT OF INVITING

Meet Gene. He is a follower of Christ. In fact, according to his pastor, he is one of the most committed disciples in his church.

"Gene is very consistent in his walk with Christ," the pastor shared. "You can count on him to do the right thing and to make the commitments that help our church have a stronger gospel presence in the community."

The pastor continued, "To be honest, I haven't known

many people like Gene. He has a strong desire to help others, and he has a passion for sharing the gospel."

Gene became a Christian in his forties, after a coworker invited him to a church worship service. Not only did the coworker invite Gene to church, but he also invited him to lunch afterward. Gene had recently gone through a painful divorce, so he welcomed the company of his Christian friend.

From that point, Gene started attending worship services regularly, and he joined the community group his coworker attended. No one was really surprised when Gene decided to become a follower of Christ. Many, though, were surprised by his rapid spiritual growth.

Three years have passed since Gene was invited to church. He has become a spiritual leader in the congregation. He shares the gospel in the community. He invites people to church. Many of those have become followers of Christ as well.

It began with a simple invitation from his Christian coworker.

Several years ago, our Church Answers team conducted a research project about people who were not active in church. Most were not Christians. (You can see all the research in my book *The Unchurched Next Door.*) Among the many surprises, we found that nearly three out of four unchurched persons said they would attend a worship service if they were invited.

Let that number sink in.

Three out of four unchurched respondents said they would go to church if they were invited.

Though the research is now several years old, we have significant anecdotal evidence for the ongoing importance of inviting someone to church. The response rate continues to be strong.

Gene's story is just one of those stories. The Holy Spirit used one person to invite a hurting friend to church. Now that man is on fire for Christ. Now that man is inviting others and telling them about Christ.

Many times a simple act of inviting will make an eternal difference. The person you ask could be like Gene, just waiting for someone to take the initiative.

Be that individual who doesn't hesitate to invite someone else to church.

EMPOWERED BY PRAYER

It was not just an ordinary prayer meeting. Peter and John had just been released from jail by the leading priests and elders and had returned to rejoice with the other believers in Jerusalem (Acts 4:23). The early followers of Jesus knew they must share the gospel. They knew that Jesus' last words on earth were a command to be witnesses (Acts 1:8). But they also knew the only way they could have power was to depend on the Holy Spirit through prayer.

They prayed for courage to be witnesses in a hostile culture. They prayed for boldness in preaching the gospel. They prayed for power. Luke, the author of Acts, recounts what happened at the conclusion of this prayer: "The meeting place shook, and they were all filled with the Holy Spirit. Then they preached the word of God with boldness" (Acts 4:31).

They were witnesses to the life-changing power of God. They went forth with confidence because God answered their prayers.

We cannot separate evangelism from prayer. We must not attempt to witness in our own wisdom and power. Prayerless evangelism bears little fruit. Prayer-filled evangelism bears a surprising abundance of fruit.

How then do we pray to become better witnesses? Here are some suggestions:

- *Pray for opportunities.* Consider waking up with this prayer every morning: "Lord, please bring people into my path today with whom I may share the love of Christ." I've heard incredible stories from people who regularly pray that prayer. One friend told me, "I'm not sure whether God is putting people in my path or just opening my eyes to those already there, but it has become a blessing almost every day."

- *Pray for non-Christians.* As God opens your heart and eyes to the lostness of humanity, pray for non-Christians by name. Pray that the Holy Spirit will convict them of their need for a Savior.
- *Pray that people will say yes to your invitations to church.* The story I told earlier about Gene is a story that has been repeated in the lives of many people for many years. Once someone accepts an invitation to church, he or she will likely be exposed to the gospel in several ways.
- *Pray for your own boldness.* I am an introvert. I find it challenging to carry on a normal conversation with some people, let alone share the gospel with them. But God has given me boldness again and again, even when I think I can't do it. It is his power and not my own.
- *Pray for your pastor and your church leaders to be witnesses.* By the nature of their vocation, pastors and church leaders often have numerous chances to share the gospel with others. Pray for them to discern those opportunities and be bold when they recognize them.

These are only a few examples. Pray that God will give you greater insight about praying to be a better witness.

DISCUSSION QUESTIONS

1. Why is John 14:6 so important to understanding the priority of being a witness for Christ?

2. How is inviting someone to church a great way to open the doors for evangelism?

3. If you began praying to become a better witness, what are some specific things you would ask for from God?

6

I AM A PRAYER WARRIOR

I grew up going to the Florida Gulf Coast every summer. My dad didn't want to vacation anywhere else. Our family loved the place, and we loved the people. So when, during my final year of seminary, I received a packet of information from a church in St. Petersburg that was looking for a pastor, I was excited. They were just seeing if I might be interested.

Yes, I was indeed interested. Though all my vacations growing up were on the Florida Panhandle, and St. Petersburg is not, it was nevertheless on the Gulf Coast. Moreover, Pinellas County had a population of 850,000, and more than 90 percent did not go to church. So St. Pete was both a slice of paradise and a mission field.

The church itself was a different story. Attendance had

declined precipitously. Finances were in such bad shape that they could barely pay me a living wage. This was an especially difficult challenge for my family of five.

The head of the search committee was surprised I was interested. In her second letter, she said, "I really can't figure out why you are interested in our church."

At least she was honest.

A few weeks before I began my ministry at the church, I met Lillian. Her official position in the church was "prayer ministry coordinator," but the title did not do justice to the work she was doing.

Lillian and a few other members had begun praying for me even before I was a pastoral candidate. She told me she prayed for the church and me every day, sometimes several times a day. Sometimes she spent hours at the church just praying.

Rarely have I seen such a fervent person of prayer. Rarely have I been so moved by the power of prayer. Rarely has a pastor been more blessed by the prayers of a church member.

The church grew. In fact, it grew significantly. Many people became followers of Christ. The impact we had on the community was remarkable. The excitement was palpable. The unity was unmatched. Members and former members of the church often refer to my tenure there as "the glory days."

But I know better.

There is no false modesty in me when I say that I had

hardly anything to do with what happened. In fact, my primary effort was to get out of the way. I saw what God will do when his people pray. I saw how God answers prayer. I received the precious gift of a prayer warrior to her pastor and the church.

Those were indeed glory days, but without question the glory was all God's.

THE WARRIOR IN ALL OF US

The term *prayer warrior* is a curious phrase to some. The first time I ever heard it was from Lillian herself. It seems to combine militaristic language with the sacred act of prayer.

I guess the term fits.

The apostle Paul uses similar language to describe the spiritual battle we're fighting:

> A final word: Be strong in the Lord and in his mighty power. Put on all of God's armor so that you will be able to stand firm against all strategies of the devil. For we are not fighting against flesh-and-blood enemies, but against evil rulers and authorities of the unseen world, against mighty powers in this dark world, and against evil spirits in the heavenly places.
>
> EPHESIANS 6:10-12

We are indeed in a battle—a real and powerful spiritual war. Paul tells Christians to put on the full armor of God and then pray. And he doesn't tell us to pray for only a few minutes; he tells us to pray continuously.

> Pray in the Spirit at all times and on every occasion. Stay alert and be persistent in your prayers for all believers everywhere.
> EPHESIANS 6:18

As a final note, Paul asks the believers in the church at Ephesus to pray for him as well.

> Pray for me, too. Ask God to give me the right words so I can boldly explain God's mysterious plan that the Good News is for Jews and Gentiles alike.
> EPHESIANS 6:19

You get the picture. Prayer is important. In fact, it is our spiritual weapon as we fight for and along with God in this great battle.

You are in a battle. You are a prayer warrior.

PRAYING FOR YOUR WITNESS

Prayer is the power behind all successful evangelism. Indeed, evangelism without prayer is powerless. Prayer opens the door for opportunities to witness to others. Prayer unleashes the Holy Spirit to give us the right words to say when we share the gospel. Look again at this verse from the previous section: "Ask God to give me the right words so I can boldly explain God's mysterious plan that the Good News is for Jews and Gentiles alike" (Ephesians 6:19).

Paul prays for the words to be a witness, and he prays for boldness. So should we.

PRAYING FOR YOUR PASTOR

Imagine a pastor receiving a text message just minutes before he is to preach. Earlier in the service, he announced the addition of a new staff member, and the church celebrated—well, at least most of the church did. One member decided to text the pastor objecting to the new staff member's title.

The pastor receives the text and then gets up to preach. Imagine how discouraged and disheartened he feels as he takes the pulpit. For a pastor, the critics never stop, and their timing can be awful.

This pastor, like hundreds of thousands of other pastors, receives an unending stream of criticisms, suggestions, and comparisons. It never stops, and it is always discouraging.

We can't stop the critics, but we can pray for our pastors. We can pray for their strength, wisdom, and grace.

We can pray for our pastors as they bear the emotional

toll of pastoring. They celebrate births, but they bury friends. They see marriages grow, and they see marriages fall apart. They see people become followers of Christ, but they see people fall away into sin. They see the church grow, and they see the church decline. They have mountaintop moments when they preach, and they plummet into valleys when it seems their sermons have fallen on deaf ears.

"It's an emotional roller coaster that sometimes I ride once a week," one pastor told our Church Answers team. "But sometimes I ride it several days in a row. It's exhausting."

You have been called to be a prayer warrior for your pastor. Start by praying for the preaching ministry. Pray for your pastor's sermon preparation. Pray that your pastor's delivery will be blessed and used by God.

Not many people are expected to speak between fifty and a hundred times a year like a pastor is. And as if the act of speaking that often were not arduous enough, a pastor is called to speak and preach God's Word.

Pray fervently that the Word of God will go forth with power.

Pray for your pastors in the multiple roles they have—counselor, arbitrator, parliamentarian, evangelist, business-person, janitor, chaplain, and many others. Pastors cannot function in their own strength, power, and wisdom. Pray that God will give them these things and more.

Lillian was my prayer warrior in St. Petersburg. I could

not have led that church without her faithful intercession in prayer.

Frances was my prayer warrior when I served at a church in Birmingham. Incredibly, she organized more than one hundred people to pray for me at noon every day. She asked them to pause for just a few seconds and pray for their pastor. They did. I could tell. Indeed, those were some of the most powerful days in my life and ministry.

Several times in the New Testament, the apostle Paul asks local churches to pray. For example, he makes this request of the church at Philippi: "I know that as you pray for me and the Spirit of Jesus Christ helps me, this will lead to my deliverance" (Philippians 1:19). Paul knew he could not lead churches without their prayers. Your pastor also needs your prayers.

It might be the greatest gift a pastor could receive from you.

PRAYING FOR THE LOST

"Lord, I pray that if anyone here does not know you as Lord and Savior, that this will be their day of salvation."

I heard one deacon pray this same prayer almost every week. To be clear, I don't want to judge him or his prayer, but I do wonder why I never heard him share the gospel with anyone. I wonder why he persistently prayed that prayer but seemingly never asked God to lead *him* to talk to others about Jesus.

Jesus entered Jericho and saw a man named Zacchaeus in a sycamore-fig tree. He had climbed the tree to see Jesus above the crowd. Zacchaeus was one of the least popular people in town. In fact, he was the chief tax collector for the entire region, so his unpopularity was widespread.

When Jesus saw Zacchaeus and told him to come down from the tree so he could be a guest in his home, the crowd did not like it: "The people were displeased. 'He has gone to be the guest of a notorious sinner,' they grumbled" (Luke 19:7).

But when Jesus heard the words of his critics, he responded, "The Son of Man came to seek and save those who are lost" (Luke 19:10).

Do you grasp the importance of these words? Jesus made it clear that his mission was to save the lost. Our mission as a church is to do the same work today, as Christ's ambassadors. We must pray, and we must share the gospel. The two actions are inseparable.

I would rejoice if every church focused its prayer ministry on the lost. Sadly, that is not the case in many congregations. But you can be a part of the solution. Even if no one else prays along with you, you can pray for your church and its members to reach the lost. You can pray specifically for the lost by name.

Indeed, we don't hesitate in most of our churches to pray for the physical needs of members by name. But we rarely pray for those who face eternal separation from God.

Be a prayer warrior. Pray for the lost.

PRAYING FOR THE HURTING

No matter how many years pass, those who have lived through the COVID pandemic will never forget it. It has affected people physically, emotionally, and spiritually.

There were, however, many positive responses to COVID. And a lot of them came from churches. These churches learned anew the power of prayer.

A pastor in Texas shared with us that most of his members didn't know the people who lived in their neighborhood. He admitted that he himself had limited contact with people in his immediate community.

Then the pandemic hit. His church, like most churches, went into a period of quarantine. Though they livestreamed their worship services, the in-person services came to a grinding halt.

One church member decided to visit the neighborhood's social media page. She offered to pray for anyone who asked. The response was immediate and profuse. In fact, so many neighbors asked for prayer that she had to enlist other church members to help pray.

Soon the church launched a prayer ministry to respond to and follow up with the prayer requests. They moved the prayer requests page to the church website, and the requests continued to pour in.

"Pray for my husband. He's in the ICU."

"Pray for me. My company just laid me off."

"Please pray. I am fighting depression. I need help."

"I don't want this made public, but my marriage is falling apart. Please pray for me."

"I'm so afraid of what's going to happen next. We've had one battle after another during this pandemic. I just don't know if I can keep going."

"I am too old, and I am afraid to go out and get some groceries."

You get the picture. The tragedy of the pandemic birthed a powerful prayer ministry at the church. But the church members did much more than pray. When there was a need, they did everything they could to meet it directly. The elderly lady who needed groceries got two bags delivered to her porch each week. A Christian counselor met by Zoom with dozens of the neighbors. When possible, church members raised funds to help those in dire need.

When the pastor saw what God was doing through the members, he provided key leadership to keep the ministry going when the church began to regather.

Of course, the regathered church welcomed neighbors who decided to visit the church that had prayed for them. The church found a need during the pandemic and prayed for the hurting. And they quickly discovered that needs did not end when the quarantine ended.

The church is now known in the community as "the church that helps the hurting."

It began with prayer. It continues with prayer.

PRAYING FOR UNITY

My first church consultation was an accident. Perhaps I should say that I didn't know it was a church consultation. A fellow pastor in the community asked me to help him understand why his church was declining. The issue was obvious: The demographics in the church did not look like the demographics in the community.

Defining the problem was easy. Finding the solution was another matter.

The essence of the challenge was getting church members to agree on anything—specifically any plan that addressed the problem. I was in one meeting with many members of the congregation where a verbal fight broke out. The search for a solution was becoming a new problem. It was disrupting the unity of the church.

In God's power, a church can do anything if it is united. But a church can't do anything if it's not united, because God does not honor disunity.

After nearly four decades of ministry, including hundreds of church consultations, I am convinced that the church's greatest need is unity, specifically unity in the Spirit.

I made a similar statement to a group of church leaders during a consultation. One of the key leaders said that he was all in favor of church unity as long as the members met certain conditions. In other words, he would love a unified church that did everything the way he wanted.

Ouch.

Contrary to the leader's statement, a willingness to embrace unity means we are willing to give up our preferences, or at the very least put the needs and preferences of others before our own. The style of the music in the worship service. The decor of the facilities. The length of the pastor's sermons. The approach to small groups. The ministries funded in the budget. The order of the worship service.

You get the point. More times than not, decisions in churches are not do-or-die doctrinal issues. Instead, they reflect the members' preferences and desires.

When Paul wrote his letters to different churches, he often made pleas for unity. He knew that the unity of a church would largely determine its power and effectiveness.

Writing from a prison cell, Paul literally begs the church at Ephesus to be unified:

> Therefore I, a prisoner for serving the Lord, beg
> you to lead a life worthy of your calling, for you
> have been called by God. Always be humble
> and gentle. Be patient with each other, making
> allowance for each other's faults because of your
> love. Make every effort to keep yourselves unified
> in the Spirit, binding yourselves together with
> peace. For there is one body and one Spirit, just as
> you have been called to one glorious hope for the
> future.
> EPHESIANS 4:1-4

How, then, do we live in light of this mandate?

First, we must clearly grasp that we are not Lone Ranger Christians. When Paul wrote to fellow believers, he was writing to either a congregation or a leader of a congregation. Being part of a local congregation is vital. You can't have unity in the church if you are not in a church.

Second, put others before yourself. At the risk of redundancy, remember that 1 Corinthians 13, the "love chapter," was written specifically to implore the struggling congregation in Corinth to unify in love.

Finally, pray for unity. Pray that you will sacrificially

pursue unity yourself. And pray that the church where you serve will be unified as well.

We may not fully grasp God's ways, but the local church, with all its flaws, is the locus of his mission on earth until Christ returns.

The Jerusalem church, the first church in history, began with total unity. They devoted themselves to the teaching of God's Word. They enjoyed sweet fellowship together. They gave abundantly to the church and to one another. And they prayed together. When differences arose over the treatment of some church members in need, the leaders gathered the church and solved the problem in a spirit of unity (Acts 6:1-7).

The result? Those on the outside looking in saw a unified church. Consequently, they were drawn by the Spirit to the church and soon to salvation in Christ. The early churchgoers were "all the while praising God and enjoying the goodwill of all the people. And each day the Lord added to their fellowship those who were being saved" (Acts 2:47).

May it be so in our churches as well.

DISCUSSION QUESTIONS

1. Explain why the term *prayer warrior* is rich in biblical truth.

2. Think of three ways you can pray for your pastor this week.

3. Why should we pray for unity in the church?

7

I AM A CHRISTIAN

I am a Christian.

Four words. Four powerful words.

When I talk about what it means to be a Christian, I must begin with what Christ has done for me. That point is clear. I have been given a gift I don't deserve.

> God saved you by his grace when you believed. And you can't take credit for this; it is a gift from God. Salvation is not a reward for the good things we have done, so none of us can boast about it.
>
> EPHESIANS 2:8-9

I am a Christian because Jesus saved me.
I am a Christian because he died on the cross for me.

I am a Christian because he rose from the dead and defeated death for me.

If you can say, "I am a Christian," then all these truths apply to you as well.

Sometimes, though, when we memorize Scripture, we end at Ephesians 2:9. There is much, much more.

After making it emphatically clear that we are Christians only because of the work of Jesus on our behalf, Paul continues, "For we are God's masterpiece. He has created us anew in Christ Jesus, so we can do the good things he planned for us long ago" (Ephesians 2:10).

Don't miss it. We were saved not *by* our good works, but to *do* the good works that God has planned for us. We are Christians because of what Christ has done for us. We respond by growing as Christians and doing what God desires. We are not content to remain idle. In God's power, we are meant to do great things.

And there's more—a further point that is often overlooked. Yes, we are saved by grace through faith. Yes, we are saved to do good works. But we are saved to do those good works in the context and accountability of the local church.

For some reason, the place and importance of the local church in our Christian growth are often overlooked. In the book of Ephesians, Paul isn't writing to a group of anonymous Christians; he is writing a specific letter to a gathering of people—a local church—in a city called Ephesus.

There is no doubt that Paul presumed the "good things" believers would be doing would be with and through the local church in Ephesus. We simply cannot overlook that reality.

Our Church Answers team works with local church leaders around the world. We hear many stories of struggling churches, divided churches, and congregations on the precipice of closing. Consequently, these church leaders are often hurting, weary, and defeated.

But there are other churches that are thriving. Their church members are committed. Those members understand that they are meant to live out their faith before the world in the context and accountability of their local church. They proclaim enthusiastically, "I am a Christian, and I am a church member." Though church membership doesn't save anyone, the context of the local church is where God intends for Christians to flourish, serve, and evangelize. Those two "I am" statements are inextricably connected.

What then is God's plan for you? Of course I cannot know the specifics of his calling on your life, but I can say with the assurance of Scripture that your growth as a Christian will be commensurate with your growth as a committed church member.

Do Christians today grasp the incredible joy of living out their faith in a local church? We should. Three of the greatest manifestations of the Christian life can be found in our local congregations.

A GREATER FAITH

Those who were saved at Pentecost in Jerusalem quickly formed a church. In fact, Luke's narrative in Acts 2:41-47 portrays the formation of the church as almost immediate: "Those who believed what Peter said were baptized and added to the church that day—about 3,000 in all" (Acts 2:41).

It is fascinating to note that the 3,000 immediately became a church. The supernatural work of the Holy Spirit moved these new believers into a community of believers.

It was in this context that the believers demonstrated their faith. They demonstrated their faith with great boldness (Acts 4:29, 31). They demonstrated their faith as they witnessed miraculous signs and wonders (Acts 4:30). They demonstrated their faith as they gave cheerfully of their own possessions (Acts 4:32). And they demonstrated bold faith as they shared the gospel and the power of the Resurrection with others (Acts 4:33).

Something powerful takes place when God's people come together in faith. It happened two thousand years ago. And it is still happening today.

Something exciting takes place when Christians renew their commitment to Christ. Inevitably, they also renew their commitment to a local church. They intuitively understand that a committed Christian is also a committed church member. They demonstrate that the faith they have in Christ is a faith lived out in the community of believers.

A GREATER HOPE

I love my local church's vision statement. It is simple but powerful: "We exist because everyone needs the hope of Jesus."

I recalled in an earlier chapter how my growth in Christ did not begin until I connected with a local church. A life issue—my wife's pregnancy—prompted the move, along with my wife's gentle nudging.

I also recalled how the first ministry project of our men's Bible study affected me profoundly. I will never forget the look on the face of that single mom when we made her Christmas an incredibly joyful event. I saw hope on display!

But I noticed something else about my Christian walk when I connected with a local church. Not only was I part of a greater group dispensing hope, but I was also the recipient of hope. It was not until I committed to a local church that I fully understood what Christian hope really is.

True hope, for certain, begins with Christ. But hope also comes from the community of believers with whom we connect on a regular basis.

I can anticipate the objections: The church is full of

hypocrites. The church is not led well. I can't worship at my church. Money is spent in the wrong places.

I get it. Every objection has some validity. But no objection should keep us away from growing as Christians through the ministry and life of a local church.

You're no doubt familiar with the story of the woman caught in the act of adultery and brought to Jesus by the Pharisees in John 8:1-11. On the one hand, I love how Jesus interacts with the woman, forgives her, and tells her to go and sin no more. It is a snapshot of grace at its fullest.

But I find myself drawn to the Pharisees, who are ready to pick up stones and kill this woman according to the law of Moses. How many times have I looked at other sinners and wanted to judge them? How many times have I been frustrated or angry with a church member for something they did or said?

In those moments, I am a Pharisee. I have a stone in my hand.

But then I am pulled back to Jesus. I see his love. I see his compassion. I see his hope. It reminds me that I am to be a conduit of hope for those who are not yet Christians. It also reminds me that I am a conduit and recipient of hope in my local church.

God's design for his church is that its members will bring hope and encouragement to one another. When this happens, it is an amazing thing to see.

A GREATER LOVE

In 1 Corinthians 13, the Greek word for "love," repeated eight times in thirteen verses, is *agape*. It is the same word used in the Gospels to describe the love of God (see, for example, Luke 11:42; John 5:42; John 15:9-10, 13).

Agape is emphasized in the midst of significant conflicts in the Corinthian church. Paul, in writing 1 Corinthians, emphatically states that we are to love others. Patient love. Kind love. Love that isn't jealous. Love that doesn't boast. Love that isn't prideful. Love that isn't rude. Love that doesn't demand its own way. Love that isn't irritable. Love that keeps no record of wrongs. Love that rejoices when truth wins out. Love that never gives up. Love that never loses faith. Love that is always hopeful. Love that endures through every circumstance.

It is an unconditional love. It is *agape* love.

It is the type of love we should have for one another. It is the type of love we should have for those in our local church.

By the way, "three things will last forever—faith, hope, and love—and the greatest of these is love" (1 Corinthians 13:13).

I AM A CHRISTIAN, AND I AM NOT ALONE.

As we've seen, being a Christian means believing in a set of biblical truths. Certainly, I cannot consider myself a follower of Christ unless I embrace the truths he gave us.

I am a believer.

Being a Christian also means following Christ in our actions. It's asking the question, "What would Jesus do?" and acting accordingly. I cannot consider myself a follower of Christ unless I have a faith that works.

I am a disciple.

Being a Christian means desiring to emulate the servant-hood of Jesus. After all, he said that he came to serve and not to be served (Mark 10:45). I cannot consider myself a follower of Christ unless I am willing to serve others.

I am a servant.

Being a Christian means obeying Jesus' commandment, uttered as he left the earth, to make disciples of all nations. I cannot consider myself a follower of Christ unless I am witnessing to what I have seen and sharing the gospel with others.

I am a witness.

We remember, too, how Jesus prayed, how he agonized in prayer, and how he pleaded with his disciples to pray. He even taught us how to pray in the verses we now call "the Lord's prayer" (Matthew 6:9-13). I cannot consider myself a follower of Christ unless I am one who prays.

I am a prayer warrior.

You may have noticed that the chapter titled "I Am a Church Member" is strategically placed between the chapters about belief and discipleship. I made this choice intentionally, as a reminder that our belief in Christ and our obedience to Christ are meant to be lived out in the community of the local church.

Many Christians today seem to have missed that biblical truth. They see church membership, attendance, and ministry as optional—or, worse, legalistic. They rightly say that belonging to a church doesn't save them, but they seem to overlook the fact that most of the New Testament after the four Gospels is written to and about local churches.

It is time to embrace the fullness of what it means to say, "I am a Christian." If you haven't already, it's time to take your place among the hypocrites and sinners seeking to love one another in the local church. It's time to serve instead of seeking to be served. It's time to grow, pray, evangelize, and carry one another's burdens in the community of the local church.

Being a Christian is not a burden or a legalistic obligation. It is an inexpressible joy, serving a Lord and Savior who gave his very life for you. It is true freedom. It is the fulfillment of your purpose here on earth.

Being a Christian, serving in a local church, is how we live out and express that joy.

I am a Christian, and I am a church member.

And I thank God that these two inextricable truths are his gifts to me.

May it be true for you as well.

DISCUSSION QUESTIONS

1. Why have many Christians in North America lessened their commitment to their local churches?

2. Why are many Christians in other countries willing to die to stay connected to their churches?

3. Give an example of a time in your life when you lived out your Christian faith powerfully in the context of a local church.

ABOUT THE AUTHOR

THOM S. RAINER is the founder and CEO of Church Answers. With nearly forty years of ministry experience, Thom has spent a lifetime committed to the growth and health of the local church and its leaders. He has been a pastor of four churches and interim pastor of ten churches, as well as a bestselling author, popular speaker, professor, and dean. He is a 1977 graduate of the University of Alabama and earned his MDiv and PhD degrees from The Southern Baptist Theological Seminary. Rainer has written numerous books, including three that ranked as number one bestsellers: *I Am a Church Member*, *Autopsy of a Deceased Church*, and *Simple Church*. He and his wife live in Franklin, Tennessee.